"Don't be fooled by the ti  beyond the selling process. in-depth, and very practical by both novice and experienc~ ~.~.~~~.~..~.~. Highly recommend this book to anyone interested in improving communication skills for any reason, personal or professional."

—Tom Ziglar,
Author of *Choose to Win* and proud son of Zig Ziglar

"In *The Language of Sales* Tom Hopkins does far more than impart sales knowledge. He takes you on a journey that will transform you and your ability to communicate, persuade, and sell. If you want to become a master salesperson, then buy Tom's new book, study it, and apply all you'll learn, starting today!"

—JV Crum, III MBA, JD, MS,
Millionaire Mindset Coach & Strategy Advisor

"I have known Andy for almost 20 years. During that time, he has brought high-level sales and leadership training to not only our staff, but also to countless agents we serve throughout the United States."

—Paul Hohlbein,
President, Builders and Tradesmen's Insurance Services, Inc.

"Selling with integrity can lead to incredible outcomes in not only your business life, but also your personal life. If you want to learn to do that from two masters, look no further than Tom Hopkins and Andy Eilers and the knowledge they have shared in this book. I highly recommend it."

—Nick Nanton,
EMMY® Award Winning Film & Broadway Director/
Producer, *Wall Street Journal* Best-Selling Author, Global
Shield Humanitarian Award Recipient

"I've benefitted from Andy's sales leadership and sales training skills for over a decade. Andy's question-based sales techniques drove our agency revenue during a particularly challenging time in the economy, and is key to our ongoing success."

—Doug Lindley,
President, First Service Insurance

"This is a wonderful book destined to be a sales classic, loaded with practical ideas you can use immediately to increase your sales in any market."

—Brian Tracy,
CEO of Brian Tracy International

"If you're like me, you've noticed that the business landscape has been changing at an accelerated rate. *The Language of Sales* is the most real and relevant approach to sales that's in touch with how people choose to conduct business today. It's impeccably researched and backed by hard-hitting examples—all based on decades of delivering results for clients."

—TR Garland,
Wall Street Journal Award Winner and #1 Best-Selling Author
of *Building the Ultimate Network*

"There's no doubt about it. Effective communication skills are the most critical tool in every salesperson's arsenal. Tom Hopkins and Andy Eilers show you how to level up your skill so you can maximize every client communication through *The Language of Sales*."

—Bert Martinez,
Marketing Consultant and Bestselling Author of *Dominating Your Mind*

"Sales are made or not made based on what you say AND how you say it. Implement the advice of Tom Hopkins and Andy Eilers in *The Language of Sales* to build stronger relationships with clients and close more business."

—Wendy Weiss,
The Queen of Cold Calling™

"Tom Hopkins is already renowned as the master of sales phraseology. This book breaks the myth of typical sales speak and clearly and powerfully provides us with a language to accelerate the success of those new to the profession of selling and to advance the effectiveness of veteran sales champions. This is a must-read for anyone in selling."

—Michael Norton,
Chief Revenue Officer, Eventus Solutions Group, President of the Zig Ziglar Corporate Training Solutions Team, Former Executive Vice President of Sandler Training

"My friend and colleague Tom Hopkins has been teaching people to speak the language of sales ever since I first became a speaker. I admire him greatly and recommend his wisdom to anyone seeking to succeed in business. Your words reflect your thinking and words you choose also shape your thinking. Let this book guide you to *The Language of Sales*."

—Jim Cathcart,
CSP, CPAE, Author of 19 books including *Relationship Selling*, Inducted into the Sales & Marketing Hall of Fame 2012

"Hopkins and Eilers have synthesized and updated the most critical points of success in selling. Whether you're just starting out or a veteran pro, put this book in your car and read it with your latte—Every. Single. Day."

—Wendy Lipton-Dibner,
MA, International Bestselling Author, President and CEO, Professional Impact, Inc.

2021

The Language of Sales

THE ART AND SCIENCE
OF SALES COMMUNICATION

Andy Eilers and Tom Hopkins

Made for Success
PUBLISHING

Made for Success Publishing
P.O. Box 1775
Issaquah, WA 98027

Library of Congress Cataloging-in-Publication data
Eilers, Andy and Hopkins, Tom
   The Language of Sales: The Art and Science of Sales
   Communication
   p. cm.
   ISBN-13: 978-1-64146-563-2 (Paperback)
   ISBN-13: 978-1-64146-409-3 (eBook)
   ISBN-13: 978-1-64146-410-9 (Audio)

To contact the publisher please email service@MadeforSuccess.net or call +1 425 657 0300.

Printed in the United States of America

Your life will grow and change depending upon the people you love and hold most dear. I dedicate this book to the true love of my life, my wife Michele. Thank you for being the wind beneath my wings.

—Tom Hopkins

Grace !
Life is meant to be
lived as if every day !!
is your last ! Cheers ..

Contents

INTRODUCTION

The language of sales is a combination of art and science. It's all about understanding people who are different from us and recognizing better ways of communicating effectively with them. It's not just about speaking the same language but communicating on the same level of understanding.

The science of psychology is involved. The science of body language is also part of selling others on our ideas, values, products, and services. Sociology plays an important part in understanding others as well as the study of cultural diversity.

The art aspect of selling is more personal, more individual. Just as no two artists will capture a tree the same way in a painting, no two people will apply their skills exactly the same way.

Every language has its nuances. So does selling. The key to success in selling is to learn as much as possible about the science aspect of selling, then to create a career, business, or life that is your artistic masterpiece.

Nearly every field of study has its jargon—language that is specific to that field. These are often words that are difficult for those outside that field to understand. Selling has its jargon, too, but what we're talking about in this book is not the jargon, but the method of communication that differentiates those who achieve massive success from those who don't. It's a lesson on how to be more like those who succeed at selling themselves, their ideas, their values, and their products.

With every human interaction, we are all selling something. There are even instances when we're selling while not directly interacting with others but performing tasks that will impact them in some way. An example of this might be in the words written for marketing pieces. Marketers "speak" to people though not always in person. How well we perform our jobs in packaging products and services that will ship to clients who have purchased them impacts the experience they have in the sales process with our company. We may never meet those clients, but we can be certain they'll receive a message about our company based on our performance. They will have an impression of us from how well we do our work. When our work is done well, we've sold ourselves and the companies we represent as being professional and competent. When our jobs are done poorly, we make negative impressions on others—even those we never interact with in person.

While learning our native tongues is important to communicate with those whom we are closest, learning the language of selling is critical to our overall success in life. In modern times, not many of us live out our lives in the same area in which we were born and raised. Because of that, we are bound to encounter people who are different from us in many ways. Knowing how to communicate well and how to listen to understand is critical to our overall happiness and success.

We don't always want to go along with the crowd or whatever someone else wants—especially if it's not in our best interests. We use selling skills to express our views in such a way as to provide viable alternatives, ones that others will want to follow or go along with, or to provide a reason why we won't be following that other crowd and doing so without offending them.

How do we learn the language of sales? The same way the great explorers learned to communicate with indigenous people they met. We begin with body language, gestures, simple words, repetition, and encouragement. Let's get this journey started!

1

WHY WE CALL
SALES A LANGUAGE

"We're trying to engage people rather than
dictate how they should be thinking."

—Neville Brody

When you think of the word "language," what comes to mind?
For many people, "language," quite simply, is a tool used to communicate with others. Merriam-Webster defines language as "the
system of words or signs that people use to express thoughts and
feelings to each other."

Our definition of the language of sales includes Merriam-
Webster's definition with the added position that the goal for
our use of language goes beyond communication to persuasion.
The language of sales is primarily used to educate others about
the value of our ideas, concepts, products, or services, and then to
generate decisions on the part of others. Hopefully, the decisions
others arrive at are the same as ours—that they will have happier

lives, more efficient and profitable companies, and greater overall success by choosing to own our ideas, concepts, products, or services. In order to communicate those points well, we need to be flexible and well-versed enough to educate others using a variety of words until we hit upon the ones that truly connect with them.

Language Fluency

How do you know that you can speak a language fluently? Is it when *you* feel comfortable with it? Or, is it when someone else understands you well enough to exchange ideas or come to an agreement? When it comes to the language of selling, we believe it's the latter. However, most often, the latter is dependent on the former.

When you're uncomfortable with the words you're using, it becomes obvious to your listeners. When they recognize your discomfort, their defenses are likely to go up, making the continuation of the conversation or sales process more challenging than when you *are* comfortable with what you're saying. This is where dedication to your craft becomes very important.

It's critical to become fluent in a language in order to comprehend how to use it most effectively. This includes the language of sales. We become proficient through study, practice, observation, and more practice. In this book, we will help you recognize communication flaws and provide suggestions and strategies to overcome them. You will do well to read and take to heart the wisdom in this book as it's based on our own experiences with selling—both traditional where we moved people to purchase products and private where we have been persuasive in our personal lives.

However, you won't develop your own fluency by reading this book. You only develop fluency through practice. Make a commitment to put into practice the advice we are providing. Try it on. Test it out with family members, friends, and associates. Practice some more. Then, test it with buyers. Observe how they respond to you. Always be on the lookout for new ways of describing what your products do for people; new ways of engaging them in conversations about your ideas.

What's Your Intent in Communicating?

Before beginning any communication, it's wise to set your intention for it. Communication is about intention and the ability to convey messages to others. For most of us who earn a living selling, our intention is to make sales, right? That's the overall big picture. However, when we break the sales process down into steps, our intentions for each step may vary.

We may desire to:

1. Make connections in such a way that others want to converse with us
2. Help others perceive us as experts in our fields
3. Draw information from others that will help us direct or guide conversations
4. Educate others with our product knowledge, experience, and expertise
5. Help others rationalize concerns about our products
6. Generate positive agreement that leads to decisions

Those six intentions are representative of the six steps in the sales process.

They are:

1. Prospecting
2. Establishing rapport
3. Qualifying
4. Demonstrating or presenting products
5. Overcoming objections or addressing concerns
6. Closing the sale or asking for the decision

Those outside of the field of sales could consider the components of the language of sales and their titles "sales jargon." Jargon is something you want to avoid if you intend to earn the income of a top sales producer. It can quickly lead to misunderstanding. You want to learn, early in your conversations with buyers, how familiar they are with your industry terminology before you say something that throws the sales process off course.

An important premise in the world of communication—especially in sales—is that a confused mind always says "no." Unless you are communicating with others who are in sales, avoid sales jargon. Avoid *industry* jargon unless you know the other parties to the conversation are well-versed in it.

Even though someone may be responsible for purchasing your type of product or service, they may not be deeply versed in the language. Or, you may be making a presentation to a group or committee in which the members have varying degrees of understanding of the more technical aspects of your products. Keep in mind that your goal is to always make the other parties feel comfortable and confident with you.

If you sell primarily in a single field, say to those in the medical arena, it is important that you learn *their* jargon. Again, the goal is to speak with them on the same level of understanding.

If teachers are your target market, do research on specific issues they face inside the classroom and out in the world. The same goes for consumers. When you sell to consumers, this can be a little more challenging because your buyers may include a mix of doctors, teachers, construction workers; people from any variety of fields. Knowing how to establish common ground with them is a critical skill to develop. You want to be able to create analogies specific to each person's understanding of the language you use.

Variations of Language

For a moment, let's compare sales language to sports and all the words, phrases, symbols, codes, and other forms of communication that are used. You must know the language of a particular sport in order to truly understand the game, right? If you are interested enough in a sport to follow and become engaged in watching it, understanding the terminology allows you to do so in a more rewarding manner. Otherwise, you may watch a sporting event with others, but won't truly engage.

As an example, in baseball, you have words like pitch, catch, hit, field, run, bunt, swing, curve, slider, knuckle, single, double, triple, homer, plate, foul, fair, safe, squeeze, and out. This isn't even all the words that are used when describing the different things that can happen in a baseball game but imagine if you were watching or attending a game and didn't know what these words meant in the context of the game. It would certainly make it difficult to follow the game enthusiastically from start to finish. You may not understand the reaction of others around you or the repercussions of certain actions on the field.

How about language in the workplace or in a particular industry? What if you were in the insurance industry, for example, and you spoke "insurance-ese" every day—a language you and your fellow "insurance speakers" all understood? Perhaps you would walk into your office one day and have your boss ask whether you are quoting a liability, worker's compensation, auto, property, inland marine, boiler and machinery, or excess policy for a client. When you understand the language of insurance, you answer quickly. When you don't understand the language, the conversation might become awkward when you asked what one or all of these means. If you don't understand a language fluently or can't speak a language or sub-language fluently, you cannot get the most out of every situation you are in.

Here is another example: Imagine going to a foreign country and trying to get by without knowing the language or putting forth the effort to speak it. Think about how much you would potentially miss knowing you couldn't communicate as easily as you do in your native tongue. You might miss some of the best sights. You may have less-than-satisfying meals. You may pay too much for something or even get lost.

Based on this premise, can you imagine trying to make a career out of something that, in order to be extremely successful, would require studying your "vocational language" every day and consciously choosing not to do it? It just doesn't make sense, does it?

Everyone Sells Something

Mastering the language of sales is critical for those of us who have chosen selling as our careers. That's a no-brainer. However, it's also critical to others as the communication skills necessary for sales easily carry over to other areas of our lives.

Here's a great example of what we are talking about. If you have children, you are constantly "selling" them on your ideas about how things should be done—about how to get along with others and how to get along in the world. You don't just let them do whatever they want. We all want our children to become upstanding citizens and valuable contributors to society, and we *sell* them on that every day through our words and actions.

How about your relatives? Do you find yourself trying to convince them of something you want to do or want them to do? How about your spouse or significant other? When you want something, and he or she wants something quite the opposite, how is that compromise or decision made? Who sells the idea better, you or that other person in the relationship? Who has stronger negotiating points? Are you able to understand how you or they do a better job of persuasion?

A perfect example of this is how politicians use language to persuade people to follow them and then to have those people vote them into office. One of your authors has often been asked to weigh in on which politician "sold" themselves better during a debate; to analyze which candidate used the language of sales most effectively. It can be quite interesting once you pay attention to their use of language—not just the points they make.

The fact remains that every one of us is in selling situations every day—literally with every human interaction. No matter what the situation, understand that selling skills can be as valuable as any other skill to make life better in a lot of ways. Think about how much better your life could be in the area of communicating with your kids if you were able to sell them on the idea of doing what would be best for them most of the time instead of having to use your authority to do so.

What about being able to sell your ideas to your brothers and sisters or parents instead of feeling like you have to follow their direction in everything you do? Ultimately, you are choosing the language of sales every single time you take a position or a stance on a topic and maintain your position.

You "sold" yourself into your current job. You were selling your personality, your attitude, your skills, and the value you could bring to the company. When you asked for a raise at your job, you were selling your value again—to the company, its clients, and your fellow workers.

The Most Important Sale

The most important sale you will ever make is to yourself. Remember these words as you think about how this affects your life going forward: "Nothing happens in life until a sale takes place."

Here's an example of how this plays out in your personal life: When you wake up in the morning, you have choices. Knowing that the choices you make are under your control and that you are responsible for them should guide you to the best ones. We all know that different choices produce different outcomes. When we understand the psychology and power of persuasive communication, we can use it 100 percent of the time—even on ourselves. After all, the only true motivation is self-motivation. Knowing yourself and what motivates you is what will allow you to make the choices that lead to even better choices, thus delivering better results.

Consider the following simple examples of selling yourself and see which choices you find yourself making each day and how they impact the results you're getting.

Option 1: When you wake up at a specified time, you sell yourself on getting out of bed with energy and enthusiasm; and doing the activities that will allow you to have all of the things you want in your life. That might include waking up a little earlier and reading, watching, or listening to some of your favorite educational, motivational, or inspirational material. It may include using affirmations, meditation, and prayer. It may involve either reviewing current goals or creating new goals and plans for that day. It would include proper diet, exercise, and getting the rest you need to be your best self, so you can complete your chosen tasks in a timely and efficient manner. It would allow you to get the most out of every day in both your personal and professional life. As a result, you have sold yourself on being the best you, and it shows in everything you do.

Option 2: You wake up tired because you didn't allow yourself enough time to properly rest, and now you are already off to a challenging start. You have to sell yourself on getting out of bed, which isn't easy because you are tired. You may not have provided the best fuel for your body yesterday and want to sleep longer. You hit the snooze button on your alarm and sleep for another 30 minutes. When you wake up in 30 minutes, you are still tired and are now also irritable. Because of how you feel, you don't communicate with loved ones as thoughtfully as you would otherwise. As a result, you are in no mood to read or learn; too tired to exercise. You skip breakfast, don't review or create goals and plans for the day, rush to get ready for work so you won't be late, and the whole rest of the day you feel like you are playing "catch up." Since you skipped breakfast, you are hungry and unable to focus. You drink too much coffee and become jittery.

You let the media or your default conditioning convince you that grabbing fast food will save time and fill you up, but then you have a *food coma* in the afternoon and feel lethargic as you sit at your desk staring at your computer instead of being productive. As a result, you are unable to complete the important tasks that you should, and now you realize that you'll be running behind tomorrow as well. You then sell yourself on the idea that you will just have to catch up tomorrow. You choose to leave those uncompleted tasks behind and head home at your regular time instead of working a little later and dealing with the hottest tasks today. After all, you need to go home and relax after this rough day and maybe unwind by watching television. On your way home, you stop by another fast food place, so you don't have to cook. Sound familiar? Hopefully not, but if it does, consider the words of the modern-day philosopher Jim Rohn that "nothing gets better in life until you do."

If any of this second example sounds familiar to you, answer this: When are you going to take control of your life, so the outcome of your efforts is exactly what you want it to be? Only you can decide that, but it starts with selling yourself on being your best every day. It also means never settling for being *good enough* when you can always improve, learn, and grow.

This doesn't mean you have to tell yourself anything that would be harmful or untrue. Everything you are going to be telling yourself every single day will be good and positive, just like your communications with buyers and clients. Use your selling skills to start training your subconscious mind to prepare your conscious mind to take positive action. When you give your subconscious mind a command, it won't decide whether it is positive or negative. It will simply start working on a way for you to carry out any command you feed it. When you give positive commands, your subconscious mind will lead you to take positive actions. However, when you feed your mind negative commands, you are setting yourself up to generate negative results.

It's important to recognize the effect of the words you use on yourself. You're careful about how your messages impact feelings, thoughts, and results when communicating with clients. Do the same for yourself.

As an example, what do you think of or feel when you think of the word "work." Is it something you want to avoid? Or, is it satisfying and rewarding to you? If you feed your subconscious mind the information that you don't enjoy what you are doing each day to earn an income, it will cause you to start seeing the negative instead of the positive. Instead, look at each day and what you accomplish as the way you're writing your paycheck not just today, but into the future. That means selling yourself in a positive way on making the most out of every day you work, so you can earn opportunities for even greater enjoyment during non-working hours. Remember, you are selling yourself every day you work even if you don't feel like you have a key role in your company at this point in your life.

Selling in the Workplace

Having the ability to sell yourself and your ideas in the work-place is powerful. It allows you to choose your personal path to success both with clients and inside your company.

Here are some examples of applying the language of sales and how it can play out for you moving forward.

- If you are a salesperson, imagine being able to educate and guide your potential clients to buying decisions more often than you do now—without getting pushy or aggressive.

- If you are a manager or company leader, imagine being able to sell your staff or team on doing what helps the company knowing that it can also help you in your career advancement.

- If you are an employee, envision selling others on the wonderful new ideas you have for creating a more rewarding workplace or generating greater results for the company so you will receive recognition and reward.

All of the above can happen with the effective use of the language of sales. It all comes down to this: When you master the communication skills and strategies in this book, you will get more "yes" in your life.

The interesting thing about people in every industry is that they often say that they aren't in sales. We know they are and want to help you recognize this too. Think about when you call into a company. When you get a receptionist on the phone trying to connect with a certain person, isn't the receptionist representing the company? Isn't the receptionist influencing you instantly by creating either a positive or negative image of that company by their tone of voice, their enthusiasm, and their desire to help? Their job is to *sell* the professionalism of the company with every person who calls. And, as a salesperson calling in to that company, aren't you trying to *persuade* that receptionist to connect you with the right person for your needs? That's totally a selling situation. (Even when you get voicemail, the message you hear influences your feelings about the company.)

Now, let's think about customer service people. When they are assisting you, they are selling you on why you should continue to do business with their company based on how well they serve your needs. This holds true through most of the positions, if not all, that a company may have. Even when someone doesn't interact with *external* clients, it is likely that there is interaction with *internal* clients. These could be bosses, co-workers, or subordinates. So, the fact is everyone is constantly selling in every human interaction—even if they are selling ideas or concepts versus actual products or services.

Now that we have established that truth, imagine if you could go back to high school when you were required to take a second language course to graduate, and "Sales" (or "Business Communications") was an option in place of Spanish, French, German, Chinese, or Sign Language. Would you take the course? We believe every student should have the option of taking such a course as it will impact their level of success for the rest of their lives.

As we move forward here explaining what sales really is, how it works, and how you can use the language of sales to improve everything you do, please keep a few important thoughts in mind.

First, the language of sales should never be used to manipulate or harm others. Many people in history have used their ability to persuade people to do things that have been extremely detrimental, but that is not what this writing is about. Scammers use very persuasive language and tactics to benefit themselves while causing harm to others. The foundation of our training is that you only use the strategies in this book to create winning situations for your clients and others with whom you engage.

Second, as you continue your journey to becoming fluent in the language of sales, remind yourself how important it is to bring positive influence to others by teaching them what you have learned. This could include your family, friends, and co-workers, as well as clients. Learn this material to make your life and the lives of others you become involved with better. When you use the language of sales to get that better table at a restaurant (or anything else in life), share the strategy with loved ones so they can enjoy greater satisfaction as well.

Third, please take this information seriously with the understanding that mastering the language of sales will create tremendous value for you personally because you will automatically do a better job of preparing yourself for everything in your life. Imagine being able to create more opportunities for yourself. Imagine waking up every single day with a positive attitude because you are armed with this information and are able to start using it with the highest level of confidence to get more wins, more yeses, in your life.

Most of all, though, imagine how much more meaningful your life will be when you are clear and focused on producing results instead of letting reasons or excuses hold you back. Dr. Robert Anthony, the author of *The Secret of Deliberate Creation*, reminds us that, "You can only have two things in life, reasons or results. Notice: reasons don't count." Make the decision today that you are only going to accept positive results in your life and are not going to allow *reasons* or *excuses* to get in your way or hold you back.

Once you understand how beneficial the language of selling is and become fluent in it, you will change your life for the better forever. You will want to use this beautifully-crafted language in everything you do both personally and professionally to have more rewarding experiences and to create, build, and keep better relationships with everyone know or will meet in the future.

2

SELLING IS SERVING

"We all have the power to influence others. It is up to us whether we are going to abuse that power to manipulate people or use it to help them."

—Abhijit Naskar

The best leaders in any field are servant leaders. Great leaders understand that they can't lead without developing followers. And, followers follow because the leader serves a need they have. It's really that simple.

Top sales leaders understand this concept and adopt an attitude of servitude with their clients. They recognize the fact that the client is in the driver's seat when it comes to analyzing and making buying decisions. The salesperson is the navigator. To serve your buyers well, adopt the following perspective with them: "Tell me where you want to go, and I'll help you find the best way to get there." You're the expert on the industry and your type of product.

You are fully capable of guiding them to their ideal destination, once you know what it is and why they want to go there.

As sales professionals, we determine what it is the buyer wants through the language we use while applying questioning strategies and first-rate listening skills. With our knowledge and expertise, we help buyers find the best solutions for their challenges with a servant's attitude.

Those who fall into the thinking associated with stereotypical salespeople that you have to approach people, take over the conversation, and talk, talk, talk, are likely only to have mediocre sales careers. When your goal is to achieve greatness in sales—having a career that takes advantage of the unlimited potential in sales—you will act and speak like the opposite of the stereotype. You'll approach every client contact with a true servant's heart.

This was never more simply expressed than by the great motivator Zig Ziglar when he said, "You can have everything in life you want if you will just help enough other people get what they want."

Where's Your Focus?

Great communication skills are powerful tools to use in both your personal life and in business. With excellent communication skills, debates are won, experiences are enhanced, values are transferred, commitments are made, and sales are closed. Using sales language correctly and effectively will allow you to influence others tremendously. The important thing to remember is to use this power wisely. True power lies in the ability to move others to actions that are in their best interests. That's selling at its finest.

Sadly, many powerful communicators in history were solely focused on their own best interests and took advantage of others. Hence, the origin of the sayings, "Once bitten, twice shy," and "Fool me once, shame on you. Fool me twice, shame on me." People learn quickly who they can trust and who cannot be trusted. When you use proper sales language, you build trust.

While having a career in selling is a means to an end, which is earning the income required to support the lifestyle you want, those who have the most successful careers focus more on helping people than on earning money. Use money and love people instead of loving money and using people. It's the only path to true success in business and in life.

In fact, one of the most important lessons in sales is to get the dollar signs out of your eyes. If you're like us, you've experienced at least one buying situation where you felt more like prey than a potential client. This happens when the salesperson operates with the mentality of "if I don't kill, I don't eat." They're too concerned about their own paychecks to care about your needs. In other words, when they sell something, it's all about what they gain. It's not at all about serving your needs.

This same premise applies when we become obsessed with getting our way in non-sales situations. We push. We plead. We demand. We hold out. And, some, like little children, throw fits. Sadly, there are those who will go along to get along and give in to that type of communication. However, the use of manipulative communication does little for building long-term careers or relationships of true value. Long-term business and personal relationships are built on attitudes of respect and service. When a buyer has a bad experience because of the methods employed by a salesperson, they are unlikely to buy from them again. Their experience could also negatively affect their opinion of the product or brand, causing them to look for a completely different product when their next need arises.

If you can, picture the record players of the past, you know that a vinyl record is placed on a turntable. Then, the arm of the player is positioned over the record, and the main point of contact between the two is a needle. If the needle isn't sharp, the sound quality cannot be great even if they are attached to the highest quality speakers in the world. In business, salespeople are the "needles." They are the points of contact. If their skills aren't sharp, it won't matter how great the product quality is. Buyers won't buy as often as they would from salespeople who have honed their skills and mastered their abilities to perform in their capacity of helping buyers resolve challenges and have high-quality experiences with the brand.

When you humble yourself to serve the needs of others, whether they're clients, loved ones, or perfect strangers, you'll do well. You will communicate to them that they're important, and that's the greatest gift you can give anyone—to show that you value them and what they have to say.

If you think about what has brought you close to others, you will likely find that it was their willingness to give of themselves before expecting you to give anything in return—if they expected anything at all.

Can you think of people like that?

Are *you* that type of person?

If you are, consider what type of influence you have in your personal and professional life as a result. Have you heard friends, relatives, associates, or clients say, "thank you" or "I owe you one" after you've listened, given advice, gotten them involved in your product, or done them a simple favor? If so, you're already using and benefiting from an attitude of servitude.

In sales, hearing a client say, "thank you" is li[k]
ing ovation for an excellent performance. You've
expected to do—serve them well. After all, th
when you hear those two magic words, you kno
their expectations in some way. And that's how trust is built.

If you know others who go about life with attitudes of servitude, you have probably already noticed the influence they have on the people they meet. People just like being around them. Being other-focused is a trait of great leaders. This has been proven over again throughout history. In fact, one of the most influential, other-focused beings who ever lived was Jesus Christ of Nazareth.

If you have read any of the New Testament or have heard the stories about Jesus and His influence, you know that He brought people closer to Him through His service to others. His ability to communicate and share while serving was never about putting Himself on a pedestal, but rather about teaching others by example—that operating from a place of humility and love for others is the way to go. Humility is a trait that is greatly valued even now, over two thousand years after His teachings were first delivered.

In the 20th century, self-help author Napoleon Hill was known to say, "Success without humility of heart is apt to prove only temporary and unsatisfying." What happens when we start to achieve success in any endeavor is that there's a tendency to become prideful. It's important to be proud of our accomplishments, but to temper that sense of pride with humility. It's not a matter of thinking less of yourself. It's about thinking of yourself less of the time. Be other-focused.

Isn't Selling

If you ask the next five people you meet to describe someone who is in sales, most will say, "They're big talkers." That's largely due to the stereotypical salesperson portrayed on television and in the movies. We're here to inform you that *telling isn't selling*. When you're speaking, you're delivering a message. That message is based on your existing knowledge, isn't it? After all, you can't speak to something you don't have knowledge about. Well, maybe some unprofessional salespeople will profess to have knowledge they don't, but that's not you, is it? Your standards are such that you speak the truth, and if you don't know the answer to a question, you admit it and offer to do research to find the answer.

In some situations, "talking and telling" may be required, but certainly not in all instances, and frankly not even most. What makes more sense when you think of selling someone on something you believe to be good for them is to be able to approach them as if you were looking through their eyes at their current situations. Your goal should be to understand *their* perspective about whatever challenge they're facing and to look for a solution alongside them.

There's a story about a real estate agent who was blind. This man achieved greatness in his field—winning awards for the volume of sales he completed. When asked about how he did so with his "handicap," his reply was that he wasn't handicapped at all. Because of his blindness, he had an advantage over sighted agents. He didn't prejudge anyone or any property by appearance. He focused simply on the needs expressed by his buyers and helping them find what *they* were looking for. He never had an opinion on properties because he couldn't see them.

If you picture a typical selling situation, most often, the buyer and salesperson face each other. This can, in some cases, be considered an adversarial position. When selling one-on-one, try to get into a position of working alongside the buyer—working together to find a solution that's, once again, good for them. You're not the adversary trying to pull money out of their pockets. You're an expert on your product and industry whose goal is to educate buyers, so they can make wise decisions. Once you accomplish that *positioning,* you are providing those you serve with a non-stereotypical approach.

If telling isn't selling, what is? Selling involves the process of asking questions, evaluating the answers, and then, and only then, "telling" or demonstrating the solution you would recommend based on your actual knowledge. Avoid the belief that you know what's best for others, without investing the time and effort in communication to determine if that's true.

Some salespeople are afraid to ask questions. They fear losing control of the conversation when the buyer is talking. This fear causes them to worry, "What if the buyer goes off-topic?" "What if they start talking about something I want to cover later in the presentation?" "How do I keep control of the presentation?"

Remember this: The person who is asking the questions controls the direction of the conversation. That's one of the most important points about the language of sales. When you become what is called a "master asker," you will calmly and smoothly control the entire sales process. You will be an expert communicator. You will demonstrate such professionalism that your buyers will follow your lead.

Our goal is that you help us change the perception of stereo-typical, "what's in it for me" salespeople to that of "salespeople are professional problem solvers." That's really what we do, isn't it? We keep abreast of the latest developments in our industries. We stay current on company and product information. We learn from every client how *they* benefit from our products and services. With our constantly improving expertise, we serve our new and existing clients better and better.

The pros often learn the best questioning strategies by working backward from the point of sale. They begin by asking themselves a series of questions:

1. How do I ask for the sale once I determine my product is right for the buyer?
2. How do I convince the buyer that my product is right for him or her?
3. How do I determine my product is right for the buyer?
4. What questions do I ask in order to get the information I need to determine if my product solves buyer challenges?
5. What are the most common challenges my product overcomes?

Do you see the pattern here? As a sales pro, you know the answer you want to get—a closed sale. Your challenge is to discover the questions and conversations that lead up to it.

Beware of Sale-Killing Questions

Be careful when asking questions that you don't ask anything the buyer can't answer. How does someone feel when you ask them a question they don't know the answer to? How would you feel if someone came into your office for an appointment and said, "We have three types of machines: Our G Series with plotting and printing capability, our E Series that's plug-in programmable for over two hundred functions and operations, and our Super Z Series that features microgrid diffraction reduction and accepts add-on modules for simultaneous QKD input. Which series are you interested in?"

Do you think the buyer will say, "Listen, I don't have a clue as to what you just said. Give me whatever you think is best. Here's my checkbook. Fill one out, and I'll sign it." Think again.

In order to feel out whether you're being too technical, build questions that give you those answers you need on your checklist we discussed earlier. Buffer these questions with phrases such as, "Are you familiar with..." or "Have you ever worked with ..." Simple, non-threatening questions about their level of understanding will help you go a long way in winning potential customers over.

Remember, words create pictures, and if a word paints no clear picture for your client, you may lead them to confusion, which will, in turn, create a barrier between you and them.

Egos are a fragile thing. One careless word or phrase can damage your presentation beyond repair. Then all you have managed to do is the time consuming and expensive preliminary work for a truly professional salesperson who knows the value of proper questioning techniques. Your slightly educated, lost customer will warm up quickly to another salesperson who knows just how to handle them at their level. Isn't it more profitable to learn to use these methods yourself?

The professional salesperson's road is so much smoother when the customer's interest and curiosity have already been piqued by the failures of average salespeople before him. Don't spend all your time planting, only for someone else to come along and harvest your crop. Be the leader. Learn how to achieve success through the use of strong questioning methods.

Andy

I remember helping a particular client when I was working as the Director of Sales with a large commercial insurance agency. We were looking for an opportunity to offer professional insurance services to a large residential remodeling contractor in Northern California.

When I first contacted the remodeling contractor, he told me that he would like to meet and learn more about what we do. He wanted to see how our agency's products and services would compare with his current agency and others he had met with. What I remember that reminds me of the importance of learning about the client before attempting to sell might surprise you.

With commercial insurance, especially when it comes to policies with carriers in the construction arena, many of the policies have unique features that can either significantly help or harm the client if they don't really understand their policies. As is the case with most people I encountered in that industry, taking the time to read and truly understand a commercial general liability policy is not always a top priority and seldom takes place. In this case, the original agent had failed to explain what would end up being a key aspect of the policy that allowed me to quickly create an incredible opportunity.

When I first met with the potential client, he told me that he might already have enough agents looking at his account and may not need another quote. Right then, I had to make one of two decisions: 1) Was our conversation going to be about him and his company, serving both, and could I simply provide expertise with no guarantee of earning his business? Or, 2) was it going to be about me and only serving him if I was thinking there was a way to earn his business?

At that time, he still had about two months left in the policy period. By asking him several questions instead of trying to sell him on why he should let me join the group of people offering a proposal for his commercial insurance, I learned that his business was not on track to hit the sales numbers that his policy premium was estimated on 10 months prior. What that meant was that he was going to overpay for the next policy based on those estimated numbers if the policy ran the full 12 months. He had no idea that this was the case, and I didn't immediately bring that to his attention as I was still in the exploratory stage of our initial meeting.

We were communicating in a way that was not about selling, but rather learning and exploring the opportunity to serve. Remember this important point as I continue. We explored everything he and his business were and were not covered for in the current policy and how that could affect current and future projects. After about an hour of questions and discussion about his and his company's needs, I had the information I needed to provide tremendous value to him without selling him anything.

I asked him, "How would you feel if I could show you a way to put $6,000 in your company's pocket right now before your policy expires and never have to worry again about being overcharged if you don't hit your estimated sales numbers?" Can you guess how he responded? If you guessed that he was extremely interested in the answer, you are correct. Remember, selling is not just about you knowing your product or service and attempting to sell it the same way to everyone. Selling is about approaching others with the heart of a servant; learning everything you can about them and their situations, and how you can make a difference for them in a way that others haven't or can't.

My product knowledge, combined with my mindset of serving others, led me to help this company receive a refund from their current carrier, write them a new policy that did not put them in that position in the future, and consequently earn all of their business, which generated over $500,000 in annual premiums.

The most important takeaway from this story is that even when we hear things like, "We already have enough people looking at this for us," or "We don't need any help with that right now," or "We are happy with our current supplier/ agent," you never know what might cause that mindset to change until you ask questions with the intent to serve.

Using the Language of Sales in Personal Situations

Success in sales is about being open to taking whatever time is necessary to understand others first before asking something of them. Imagine if you used that approach in every single contact you make. This isn't just about your professional life but will serve you in every area of your life. You have the choice to give information to others or to use a better approach, which is to learn all you can about their thinking and what they need before "telling" them what you think or know. That will always serve you better than going into a situation with the intent to sell your ideas, choices, and desires no matter what.

Everything we want in life, which includes the most powerful relationships we will ever build, starts with asking, not telling. We set our egos aside to learn, understand, and ultimately give, even sacrificially at times, to make the lives of others better and more fulfilling. Think of the last experience you had where you either made someone else feel amazing by giving of yourself or when someone else did that for you. We remember these times and experiences fondly because we remember that we cared for someone else or that person cared for us without expecting anything in return.

Consider what takes place when you are having a conversation with a friend, a co-worker, a love interest, your spouse or significant other, or your children. When you are more interested in learning about what is important to them rather than telling them what is important to you, doesn't that create the best learning opportunity? In fact, doesn't that lead you to be able to better convey what you might be searching for from that interaction and create the best path to obtaining it? It does. And that is the foundation of selling.

Andy

When I was growing up, many of the people I knew in high school were experimenting with drugs and alcohol. We all see this, of course. Many are tempted to follow the crowd and try what other people try just so they are not seen as outsiders. My parents were tuned in to that when I was in my early teens and understood the temptations and peer pressures that young people feel, which can lead to poor decision making. They sat me down when I was about fourteen years old and said, "Andy, we know that you are going to have people approach you about trying all kinds of things like drugs, alcohol, etc. We understand there will be pressure, but we want you to know that if you ever feel like you want to try those things, come to us and we will talk to you about it. That way, if you do try something, it can be here, and we can make sure that nothing bad happens to you in a controlled environment. We hope you won't ever decide that you want to take drugs, but we love you and will help you through it if you do, okay?"

Imagine how much of a relief that conversation was and what I walked away with as an understanding of where my relationship was with them. Obviously, they cared enough about me to sit down with me and have an adult conversation even when I was still only fourteen years old. They treated me with respect. They demonstrated that they were more concerned about my well-being and serving me as their child rather than coming across as disciplinarians issuing threats of consequences for my potential choices. This loving, serving attitude and care they displayed not only showed me how much they loved me, but also removed the desire to feel like I would ever have to sneak around behind their backs if I did have the urge to try any of the things we talked about.

That conversation allowed me to have the freedom to choose. However, the desire to respect what they had offered me led me to not wanting to try anything at all. It was as if that offer and the loving and serving attitude behind it removed any need for me to try anything because I could see that none of it could be good for me if they had so much concern. Ultimately, I didn't drink or try drugs of any kind as a result, which I'm sure was their hope from the beginning. In fact, I didn't even try alcohol until I was 20 years old. I truly believe that without this approach and my belief in my parents that the outcome would have been different.

Wouldn't it make sense to use that approach with any type of negative temptation someone in your life might face? By showing them how much you care before telling them how much you know about something, won't they see that trusting your opinion could be better for them than giving in to pressure from others? This approach has worked well for me in many instances over the years.

When you're open to learning about the interests or needs of others, you may learn that now is not the time for them to consider what you have to offer. And, that's okay. When you are applying the language of sales toward guiding children to develop character traits, or helping a young person in a career choice, they may not be ready to act right then, but they may open up about their current thinking. That information can help you guide them further. The point remains that *asking* makes conversations go more smoothly than *telling*. Asking opens doors. Asking gets other people talking. When they're talking, you're learning, but only if you're truly listening to what they're saying.

How do we know this is true? Simple. Look at the relationships you have that just seem to flow. You enjoy each other's company. You care for them and about them. You feel cared about. You can invest time together performing complicated tasks or simply being together with no specific plans. Where does that feeling, or synchronicity come from? It comes from shared values that were revealed through communication. You're both "on the same page," as we like to say.

In sales, this is called "establishing common ground." It's one of the many steps to establishing rapport with people—something that builds trust. Like the birds, we humans tend to flock together. We like hanging out with and taking advice from others who have similar interests. Having those similar interests makes us comfortable. It leads us to believe that these other "birds" understand us better than birds from a different flock. That feeling of being understood builds trust.

Who to Serve

So, whom do we humble ourselves with? Whom do we serve? By using the language of sales, the answer is simple: Everyone! The skill of using the language of sales isn't something you would want to turn on and off. It becomes part of you. It becomes your method of communication in both your personal life and sales career. Utilizing it brings joy, satisfaction, honor, and helps to generate income faster and easier than if you were telling, pushing, or demanding anything. You become known as a person who is easy to talk with; someone who has great advice; someone others want to follow.

It may seem obvious that we serve those for whom we work: employers and clients. How about serving our business associates? What about serving the person behind you as you enter the coffee shop by holding the door for them or allowing them to go ahead of you in line? Serve others while driving in traffic. It'll reduce your stress level during rush hour.

As a humble servant, most of the people you encounter will appreciate you. You'll make them feel honored and important. And making others feel important is one of the best things any human being can do. The opposite—making another feel unimportant—is one of the worst things you can do.

The idea of bringing relief to others by caring about their needs before caring about your own will always lead you to opportunity. We believe it endears you to others. It makes you memorable. And when situations arise where your wisdom or abilities can make a positive difference for someone, they'll know to call upon you and refer you to others. This is not a new strategy. It's been effective for hundreds of years. In fact, Charles Dickens reminded us that, "No one is useless in this world who lightens the burdens of others."

Ralph Waldo Emerson said, "The purpose of life is not to be happy. It is to be useful, to be honorable, to be compassionate, to have it make some difference that you have lived and lived well."

We aren't living well when we isolate ourselves from others. It is only when we engage with our fellow human beings with attitudes of service that we can make a difference. Engaging others with questions in order to get to know their needs, wants, and desires is how you use the language of sales to improve their lives and yours.

Reflexive Questions

Before we get into an explanation of specific questioning strategies, let's talk about the proper use of techniques. The ultimate goal of any professional is to become so proficient with the tools of their trade that they barely have to think about their proper use. That goes for people in the trades, doctors, dentists, artists, technicians of all types, secretaries, CPA's, cashiers—everyone.

Think about the tools of your trade—your words, tone of voice, and body language. Your goal should be to learn to use them so well that their use becomes reflexive. In other words, you use them without having to think about their proper use.

To reach this point, you must read and comprehend the strategies. Then, you must practice using them, preferably with friends or family members. Practice until the material feels comfortable. Once you feel comfortable with it, you will find yourself using it with buyers and reaping the rewards of increased sales. The smoother the technique, the more effective it will be.

Now, let's get started on the types of questions professionals ask. Professional salespeople use two basic types of questions:

1. Discovery questions
2. Leading questions

Some highly skilled professionals may even ask a combination of both types in a single question. The question not only leads the buyer toward the decision, but it uncovers more information as well.

Too few salespeople think about what they are saying to buyers. For example, how many times have you entered a store and been asked by a salesperson, "May I help you?"

What is your reflexive reply? "No thanks, I'm just looking."

Retail salespeople ask that same tired question fifty times a day and get the same boring response fifty times a day. As a matter of fact, many buyers have heard the question so much, they often fail to reply at all. What a ridiculous waste of time and potential! The day salespeople stop asking the eternal say-no question is the day they will qualify themselves to enjoy the benefits of making more sales.

If you're in retail sales, try the words below instead:

Salesperson:	"Good morning. I work here and if you have any questions, just let me know. In the meantime, feel free to look around."
Shopper:	"Thank you. I was wondering, do you have..."

An example of an incoming phone contact would be:

Salesperson:	"Good morning. Thank you for calling. How may I help you?"
Buyer:	"Well, I was wondering, do you have..."

Sometimes the best discovery question, in the given situation, doesn't end with a question mark. It may come out as a statement, but it still gets the answer the salesperson wants. The important thing to remember is to avoid asking say-no questions. Again, the average salesperson would say: "May I quote you on your next month's requirement for T-shirts?" The buyer may reply with, "No, we have all we need."

Instead of a say-no question, ask a discovery question.

Salesperson: "Do you prefer 100 percent cotton or cotton blend shirts?"

Buyer: "Cotton blends seem to sell better."

Another example might be for a salesperson to say, "Our rates on cotton blend shirts are very competitive. Would you be offended if I send you a quote on them?"

NOTE: The way this question is worded allows them to say "no," but in this case, "no" gives you an affirmative to go ahead with the quote. Some people feel they just have to say "no." If you suspect that's the case, this is an excellent way to allow them to do so, yet still move forward in the sales process.

You will always remain in control of the questioning process if you calmly lead or guide your buyer. Asking questions is not the only focus. Listening to their response is important too. Don't forget; it's your customer's affirmative response, or their contribution of added information, that you are after.

The Porcupine Technique

If someone threw something to you and you didn't know what it was and couldn't get out of the way quickly, what would you do? If you're like most people, your reflexes will cause you to reach out to catch it, and once you realized it was something you didn't want, you'd probably throw it back. All this happens in an instant. You hardly realize what you're thinking. You're relying on your reflexes.

The porcupine technique is one of answering a buyer's question with a question of your own—reflexively. You do this in such a polite and courteous manner that the buyer ignores the fact that you didn't directly answer his or her question, and you gain added information. For example, "When can we get it?" is a common question that is perfect for this technique:

> Buyer: "Could we have it delivered by the first of
> the month?"
> You: "Does delivery by the first of the month best
> suit your needs?"

When they answer "yes," and you know you can't deliver by then, you change course in the sales process. You may suggest another solution that's more readily available. Or, if you can deliver by the first of the month, you've just learned that you're one step closer to closing the sale. Using the porcupine technique keeps you in command of the presentation by controlling the questions.

You may ask, "Won't the buyer be annoyed if I don't give them specific answers to their questions?" When your porcupine reply is given smoothly and reflexively, they usually won't. You'll simply be asking a question to clarify further what it is they're asking.

It can become annoying if you overuse the porcupine questioning method or any of the methods covered in the rest of this book. As you become more professional, you will carry with you all the skills necessary to make the sale and be flexible enough to use any skill or combination of skills as needed. The key is becoming adept at delivering them with so much warmth and courtesy that the fact you're using a sales strategy never dawns on your buyers. To them, you will simply sound self-assured and confident. When you easily and calmly respond to their questions with questions, the buyer won't be thinking, "Oh, this clever salesperson has learned the porcupine question method." They will be too busy thinking of their response.

Practice using the porcupine with your family or friends. They will help you develop this skill in an effective manner, without fear of annoying a buyer.

In any type of sales work, you'll encounter questions that you can answer "yes" or "no" to and end up with nothing. You'll also be asked to give all the information you can give without getting anything in return. The porcupine question method is a helpful tool to use while building your overall sales skills. It's a key element in the language of sales.

Let's look at two more porcupines:

Buyer:	"Does this product have one of those extended warranties?"
Salesperson:	"Is having an extended warranty important to you?"
Buyer:	"Definitely not. I think they're useless."
Salesperson:	"May I ask why you feel that way?"

We all have preconceived notions about things. Your buyer may have a preconceived notion about warranties. They may have had a bad experience with a warranty, or they may not even truly understand what warranties can do for them. Isn't it vital to find out things like that before giving your response? With this buyer, if you try to sell an extended warranty, you may kill the sale.

If the reply was, "I want all the warranty I can get." Then you know how to shape the rest of your presentation, don't you?

Their answers to your porcupine questions will tell you how far you will have to go to get the final agreement, or if they even consider the product. Using porcupines will get you information. Porcupines are also used as test closes. These are questions you would ask to test the waters—to see how close your buyer is to making a buying decision.

The Champion salesperson understands how warmly the porcupine can be used, and how important it is to ask porcupine questions with an air of warm and friendly interest. Remember, the value of the porcupine is destroyed if overused. Always deliver it in a warm, friendly tone and not with a challenging "put-up or shut-up" attitude.

The Alternate Advance Question

The alternate advance is a question that suggests two answers, both of which confirm that your prospect is going ahead. These are questions that cannot be answered "yes" or "no" but give the buyer a choice: Either choice will bring an answer that tells you they are willing to keep moving ahead.

In most kinds of sales work, it's almost impossible to finalize the sale without first getting a meeting with the buyer. Because of this, it's vital that you don't lose out on opportunities unnecessarily and get stopped before you can start. This is why a Champion would never say, "Can I come by this afternoon?"

If you were a busy executive, what would you say? "No, I've got a heavy schedule today. I'll call you when I have more time."

A professional salesperson gives the buyer two options:

"Mr. Johnson, I'll be in your area this afternoon. Which time would be more convenient for me to stop by 2:00 p.m., or would you prefer 3:30 p.m.?" The buyer will either make a choice or give you an objection. This type of question shows that you are being flexible for them.

When he or she answers, "Three-thirty would be better," you have a meeting! You got it by suggesting two yeses instead of a no. Take a look at the next one:

"Mr. and Mrs. Summers, let's set up your delivery date. Which is best for you, the first or the tenth?"
"Oh, we need it by the first."

When they've told you that, you know they are at least on their way to owning it in their minds.

If your product or service requires a deposit, put your request for it in the form of an alternate advance.

Let's look at a $20 million private jet, for example. Before you get too far in the sales process, you've qualified your buyer, haven't you? If you said: "What type of deposit would you like to put down?" Some people might pull out a $100 bill and say, "Here. I'll take the jet."

So, instead, you say, "As you know, we have a substantial investment here. Which would you prefer, a 10 or 20 percent deposit?" Which one will they choose? It doesn't matter, as long as they choose one.

So, the alternate advance is any question that gives your buyer two alternatives, and either of those alternatives confirms that they are going ahead, or if they are indifferent to both alternatives, you may have an objection to address but either way, you are still moving forward in the selling process by using effective questions.

The Involvement Question

You may already be using this question without realizing that this is an important technique with a long history of success. If the involvement question came to you naturally, great. Let your previous success with it encourage you to work this method harder.

An involvement question is any positive question about the benefits of your product or service that buyers must ask themselves after they own it. In other words, an involvement question is not a buying question. It's an ownership question. When you ask an involvement question before they own your product or service, their answer confirms whether they are going ahead. Let's try this on the owner of the business that is considering that $30 million jet.

> "Mr. Myers, will you be using the plane strictly for company business, or would you consider leasing it out?"

That's an alternate advance question, isn't it? But it's also an involvement question. Notice how the professional has worded the involvement question to point out a benefit of owning the offering. Mr. Myers can reduce the cost of ownership considerably by chartering the jet when his business isn't using it, and you want him to know about this option before he stalls the decision to invest in it. This causes him to think ownership thoughts— thoughts of what he will do *after* he owns the jet.

Involvement questions can be created for every product or service. You have a challenge, and an obligation, to develop involvement questions for your offering: A challenge because not every product lends itself to this technique with equal ease; an obligation because you can't operate at your most effective level unless you create involvement questions to help your buyers own your product or service.

Your opportunity with the involvement question, and all the other skills in this book, is to create something that leads you to fulfill your clients' needs, getting more people happily involved in your product or service, thus increasing your own personal wealth. The more service you provide, the greater chance you create personal wealth.

Tiny Questions that Build Momentum

Let's begin with what's called the *standard tie-down*. A tie-down is a question at the end of a sentence that demands a "Yes" answer. Here's an example: "Cost control is very important today, isn't it?"

If what you said represents truth as the buyer sees it, won't that person respond by agreeing? When the buyer agrees that some quality of your product or service fits their needs, they've moved closer to a positive final agreement, haven't they? The use of tie-down questions enables you to get agreement or pop an objection. If they disagree with your tie-down, you'll know to alter your course, covering that point in more depth or avoiding it entirely.

Here are eighteen standard tie-downs that you will find valuable:

Wouldn't it?	Couldn't it?	Shouldn't it?
Wasn't it?	Won't they?	Won't you?
Isn't it?	Didn't it?	Doesn't it?
Haven't they?	Hasn't he?	Hasn't she?
Aren't they?	Aren't you?	Can't you?
Isn't that right?	Don't we?	Don't you agree?

There are others, of course, but these will give you a good start. Place these at the end of your sentences, and you'll gather lots of minor yeses. Remember: Selling is the art of asking the right questions to get the minor yeses that allow you to lead your prospect to the major decision and the major yes.

Here are some other tie-down sentences. Practice the technique by filling in the blanks as you read the following sentences:

> Example: "Cost control is very important today, isn't it?"
> "Most companies in your industry are investing heavily in high-tech equipment today, _____?
> "It would be convenient to have your entire team on a company mobile plan, _____?"
> "Taking care of your family is very important, _____?"
> "They're fun, _____?"
> "It just takes practice, _____?"
> "They're becoming natural now, _____?"
> "You'd like to enjoy the best that life has to offer, _____?"
> "A professional can do several things at once, _____?"
> "With a bit of practice, tie-downs will come to you easily, _____?"
> "Tie-Downs are questions that will lead your clients toward the decision to enjoy the benefits of your product or service, _____?"
> You are a Champion, _____?"
> These are easy, _____?"

Those sentences demonstrate the use of the standard tie-down. I'm certain with a little thought, you will come up with many more for your own product or service.

The Inverted Tie-Down

For variety and more warmth, you can put the tie-down at the beginning of the sentence. Before you decide that this is too simple to practice, consider that we're talking about a tool you will use in fast and demanding sales situations. A good mixture of the tie-down types covered in this chapter won't find their way into your sales situations by accident. A Champion can smoothly weave the various tie-down types in and out of the conversations by reflex. To do this requires rehearsal.

Use these tie-down exercise sentences for inverted form practice.

Standard tie-down: "Quality is what you're looking for, isn't it?"

Inverted tie-down: "Isn't quality what you're looking for?"

The prospect may say, "Yes, quality is what I'm looking for, but price is the most important thing for me." So now you've gotten more information. Better questions yield better answers!

The Internal Tie-Down

The internal tie-down is placed in the middle of the sentence. Don't fret! This is easier than it sounds. Here's a look at the standard version, the inverted tie-down, and the internal:

Standard: "Tie-downs are easy once you get a feel for them, aren't they?"

Inverted: "Aren't they easy, once you get a feel for them?"

Internal: "Tie-downs are easy, aren't they, once you get a feel for them?" Another variation of the internal form is: "Once you get a feel for them, aren't tie-downs easy?"

To change any simple tie-down sentence into the internal form, hang a phrase on the beginning or end of it. Take the shortest of the tie-down exercise sentences, "They're fun, aren't they?" Hook a phrase on the front, and you've got a complex sentence and an internal tie-down: "Once you get used to them, aren't they fun?"

The Tag-On Tie-Down

Our last tie-down question is a great agreement momentum-builder. It's used in a variety of ways. In its simplest form, you tag your tie-down onto any statement your buyer makes that is positive.

> Buyer: "Saving time is so important."
> You: "Isn't it?"

The buyer said it, so to him or her, it's true. Without sounding repetitive, when you tie down things the buyer says that may be helpful to the sale, you are bound to get a positive minor agreement.

Here's an example of tag-along questions working off tag-on tiedowns. The buyer has come into your showroom, and the matter of color comes up:

> Buyer: "My favorite color is red."
> You: "Isn't red a wonderful color? We're offering a choice of three new shades of red this year. Would you prefer Really Red, Burning Red, or Red, Red Wine?"
> Buyer: "I think I like Burning Red. It's beautiful."
> You: "Isn't it?"

When you've trained yourself to recognize opportunities for tag-along questions, you can warmly use the proper tie-down and think about a tagalong question that will both hold the buyer's interest and lead them closer to the big decision.

Opportunities for tag-on-tie-downs come and go quickly, so training yourself to recognize them is important. As you train your ear to recognize these tie-downs, you train your mind and mouth to practice them.

Use your local talk radio station to practice your skills with tie-downs by applying them to statements the host makes. Practice all the tie-down variations. Experiment with them on your friends, family members, or anyone you meet with throughout the day until they become a habit.

Create, practice, drill, and rehearse dozens of tie-down questions that are related to your product or service. Remember to mix all four types throughout your conversations. Also, be aware that you won't want to overuse the tie-down. The frequency used in practicing and learning is not the same frequency you would use in actual conversations with clients. Overuse may hurt you. Any speech pattern, when overused, can become annoying. I'm sure you know people who continually interject sounds, words, or phrases such as: "you know," "like," "literally," and "uh" into every conversation.

Overuse of questioning methods will trigger buyer suspicions that you may not be sincere. The true key to success in applying any of the methods given in this book is in the style of delivery and blending of techniques. *You must internalize the material.* Make it a natural part of you. If you are sincere in your concerns for giving your clients the best product or service, you will do what it takes to make these strategies flow smoothly.

The Service Mindset

A service mindset leads to a level of influence that is unmatched by any other approach, which is why the top people in every industry are known and respected for going above and beyond for the people they serve. Remind yourself the next time you interact with others to pay close attention to if:

1. You are the one looking out for the other person;
2. The other person is looking out for you;
3. Both of you are simultaneously looking out for each other; or
4. Neither of you are looking out for each other.

Each type of interaction has a feeling all its own. Pay attention to which one feels most natural to you. At the end of the day, these interactions and how you approach them will decide how much influence you are able to create. If you are looking to create high levels of influence in any area of life, we suggest that you come from a place of service by asking questions, learning what is important to others, and offering to be a valuable asset in their lives. This will lead you to more and greater success in all aspects of your life.

3

DEVELOPING RELATIONSHIP TRUST
The Beginning of the Sales Process

"The longer I go about living, I see it's the relationship that is most meaningful."
—William Shatner

How do we develop strong, healthy relationships? It's a process. It takes time, effort, and we must *want to* do it. However, learning how to get along with others is not something that's often taught outside of a psychotherapist's office. And, that's sad. How to build healthy, long-term relationships should be taught at every level of our education system. Sure, the pieces of how to build relationships are presented to us in kindergarten and beyond: "To have a friend, be a friend." "Be nice to others." "Be polite." "Treat others with respect." "Live by the Golden Rule." But few put those pieces together into a cohesive training module on how to develop relationships.

Our relationships with those who care for us as babies and youngsters develop out of necessity. In some cases, like with our family members and neighbors, we develop relationships due to proximity. We share similar values, similar houses, meals, and maybe even the same hand-me-down clothes. We attend the same schools, churches, and play on the same playgrounds.

Many business relationships will develop out of necessity. Your clients have specific needs that your product fulfills. However, before that necessity can be recognized, we need to find those clients, get their attention, build their interest in us and our products, and then persuade them to act. It's quite a bit more complicated than forming neighborhood friendships, but there is a formula for doing so.

In advertising, this formula is known as the A.I.D.A. Formula. The letters stand for:

Attention

Interest

Desire

Action

That formula has been the model for advertising campaigns for decades. It's simple, yet powerful. Get the attention of your audience or potential market. Pique their interest in what you have to say. Create a desire for the benefits of your product or service. And, finally, move them to action. Those actions might include visiting your website, downloading something, making a phone call, or popping into your location. If any of the four elements are missing in your ads, the ad will likely fall short in generating results. Since this formula has been such a well-known and proven staple, we recommend using it in developing relationships both in business and personally.

Once you discover your ideal type of client—those who would receive the greatest benefit from your product or service—your next step is to get their attention. To get someone's attention, you must get in front of them or go where they are—maybe not personally, but with your advertising messages and promotions. Where do your ideal clients work? Play? Hang out? Travel? It's important to learn the answers to those questions.

If you're not sure how this works, watch an hour's worth of television advertising. Pay attention to the demographic of the people in the shows, then in the ads. Are they young? Old? Healthy? In need of medical care? From a certain ethnic or socioeconomic group? Do they have kids? Are they single parents? Are they college students? Or job hunting? Do they cook? Are they traveling? With every commercial, ask yourself, "What type of people are being targeted here?" Doing this is much more interesting than mindlessly watching and waiting for your favorite show to return.

Smart advertisers put people in their ads who are just like those they want to attract. That's because when we see someone who is "just like us" being happier, healthier, wealthier, or just having more fun, we want to be like them. We want to have whatever it is that's making their lives better. It's human nature.

Now, where are we going to find *your* ideal clients? Do you need to approach them at their place of work as in working with purchasing agents or committees in formal business settings? Or, is your product, service, or idea such that you'll meet with them in less formal settings such as at trade fairs, in their homes or the homes of friends, at recreational activities, or through media such as television commercials or billboards? If you aren't sure, think about your three best clients. How did you first encounter them? Or, even better, how did they find you? Begin there when looking for new clients.

Common Ground

The foundation of most relationships is often simply common ground. Because early relationships form because of common ground, it's important that we recognize and use that knowledge to our benefit in forming *business* relationships. It's a concept we are all familiar with. Common ground is defined as *any interest or location two or more people share.* It can literally mean the ground you're standing on, such as in a building, on a soccer field, or other *place.* Or, it can refer to a common interest such as a field of study, a sports team, or a hobby or recreational *activity.*

When we meet someone new, we don't yet know if they are someone we want to have a deeper relationship with, right? It's all surface courtesy and manners. The next thing that happens is that we either recognize or seek out common ground. Here are a few examples:

- We're both standing in line at the coffee shop. There are pretty good odds one point of common ground is that we both like (need?) coffee. Of course, there will always be those picking up coffee for others, or tea drinkers, but you get the point.

- We're both at a certain networking event. We're there to meet new people and discover how we can help them.

- We comment on the same blog post, news item, or social media post. (This is one of the most under-used strategies for finding leads. Read the other comments and reach out to those people!)

- We share industry connections.

- We live in the same city.

- We drive the same roads to work every day.

- We work in the same or complementary industries.

- We have kids of similar ages or are involved in the same sport.

- We own the same brand or type of vehicle.

- We have vacationed in the same national park or traveled to the same foreign country.

- As seen in the movies: We both try to grab the same cab during a rainstorm.

Common ground is the starting point of relationships. Pay attention to where you are and why you're speaking with someone to begin establishing common ground.

Establishing Rapport

Establishing rapport is a skill in itself for both sales and personal relationship situations. It is where you make a positive first impression and get to know a little about the other person before deciding what type of relationship, if any, this might lead to. What happens in the first few moments of this stage of the sales process lays the foundation for the future of each relationship. We all know that we don't get second chances to make positive first impressions. So, it's critical that we prepare well for each first encounter.

The definition of "rapport" is *harmonious mutual understanding; the state of individuals who are in utter agreement.* Wow! "Utter agreement." Wouldn't that be a great position to be in with your clients and your loved ones? That level of rapport may require a bit of effort to work toward, but there's always a starting point.

And, it all begins with a simple smile.

You might think it unnecessary to mention smiling when it comes to interacting with others. We don't. Pay attention for a single day to the people you encounter. How many of them include a smile when they make eye contact with you? It's rare to find many. When you do see someone with a smile, notice how it makes you feel. Then, make a conscious effort to become one of those people who strive to make the day of someone else by giving them a smile. It really does make a difference.

Next, thank people for acknowledging you or engaging with you. There cannot be too much gratitude in the world. "Thanks for coming in." "Thank you for taking my call." "Thanks for reaching out." "Thanks for replying to my message." "Thank you for providing great service." The power of gratitude is underrated. When people feel appreciated, they'll warm up to you and lower any defenses they had raised upon your initial encounter.

The acknowledgment of gratitude goes back to Biblical times, where we see the apostle Paul begins his letters to the early Christians with gratitude for those who read them. Use it generously!

Next comes the exchange of names. This may sound simplistic, but it's the nuances of selling that add up to sales or no-sales. You want to get as many of them as possible right. Pay careful attention to the names people give and only use them the way they're given.

Let's say you meet a man named Robert. Don't be quick to call him Rob, Bob, or Bert. Early in the "getting-to-know-you" stage, it's better to err on the side of formality. After you and the clients warm up a bit to each other, you may earn the right to ask if you can call people by their first names. When you use their names a few times immediately after hearing them, you'll be less likely to forget them later. Saying each buyer's name silently to yourself at least four times will prove helpful to your memory.

Tom

Early in my real estate career, I spent quite a bit of time over a weekend with a very nice couple who were searching for a home. As our time together became more relaxed, I asked permission to call them by the nicknames I'd heard them use for each other. They agreed.

When they finally decided on a home, and we began to fill out the paperwork, I knew I had to use their legal names. So, I wanted to confirm the proper usage. I asked the man, "How should we fill this out? Would you prefer "Bob" or "Robert" on the documents?" He smiled and said, "Well, Tom, I think 'Jim' makes a lot of sense since that's my name."

I had called him by the wrong name for days! He didn't correct me because he didn't really believe they'd find a home so quickly and that it would matter.

Know that there's nothing wrong with asking someone with an unusual name to clarify the correct way to say it or spell it. In fact, the origin of their name could be a way of warming up the conversation.

Another step toward establishing rapport is to give others sincere compliments. Women tend to be more natural at this. "Nice shoes," "Great bag," or "I love your earrings" are comments often heard when two or more women are together. Guys are more likely to begin their interactions with comments such as "Oh, wow, you have the latest...?" "Nice car!" or "Your team really played well last night" (when the other person is wearing or carrying something with a team logo).

Look for something generic enough to open a conversation in a polite and positive manner with everyone. The goal is to get people to like us, so they will come to trust us and want to hear what we have to say. In other words, we want them to open their minds and ears to what our opportunities can do for them.

Then, you'll want to ask questions to engage others in conversation. Initially, these would be open questions because they require more than a simple "yes" or "no" answer.

For example, if this is a potential professional relationship, you can ask:

- "What type of work do you do?"
- "What do you enjoy most about your job?"
- "Who do you follow for expert advice?"
- "How many people work at your company?"
- "Where did you go to school?" or "What did you study?"
- "Why did you choose that field of study?" or "How did you choose that line of work?"
- "When did you plan to _____?"

Notice that all the questions start with words that make them open-ended questions. These words include: Who, What, Where, Why, When, and How. They require more in-depth answers than questions that can be answered with a simple "yes" or "no."

By continuing to ask open-ended questions in a friendly way, (you don't want to seem like you are interrogating the person), you will continue to learn more about that person's situation and their values. Their answers will help you determine whether this could lead to a professional relationship.

If you determine you can develop a business relationship that's fruitful for both of you, based on the answers to your questions, great. If you determine it will not, you must decide whether it could lead to a relationship of any kind. For example, you may have a fantastic connection with the person that is more personal than professional. And sometimes that's the way it will go.

Until he learned professional selling strategies, a salesman we know would come home and tell his wife about all the interesting people he met and befriended during his days. That was great, but while he was making a lot of friends, he wasn't making any sales. He was great at establishing rapport, but not at continuing the sales process.

With some people you meet, you may operate in completely different arenas professionally, and a personal relationship is the only one that would make sense. In those cases, you can create personal relationships without worrying about jeopardizing professional relationships. And, know that most of those with whom you have personal relationships can act as ambassadors in recommending you as a potential business contact to others they know or encounter.

Do you see how establishing rapport can help you with business relationships? You can use this exact same strategy when creating personal relationships.

Values

Opening conversations with people is when you'll start to understand their values. Our values affect our thoughts, words, and actions. They are at the core of how we make decisions. They tell others what is important to us. And, they reflect how we relate to others in both personal and business relationships.

Some values that you may have or see reflected in others include:

- Enthusiasm

- Humility

- Trust

- Generosity

- Productivity

- Environmental awareness

- Persistence

Those values cross the spectrum of both personal and business applications. It's important to be able to recognize the values of others. When your values and theirs match, it will be easier to develop relationships with them.

In business situations, it's more important that your company's core values are compatible with a new potential client's values. For example, if the equipment you market doesn't meet certain sustainability standards that the client's company does, that conflict in values may cause them to dismiss you as a potential supplier.

When developing values questions, you will want to ask both open-ended and closed questions. The difference here is that you need some "yes" and "no" answers when it comes to values in order to know whether to proceed with the relationship. Closed questions allow you to get those answers, so you are not surprised further into the relationship with behaviors that you weren't expecting that could compromise the relationship.

The fact is that once you know what a person's values are, you can expect certain things to happen, good or bad. When you are honest with yourself, which we all know is not always as easy as we would like it to be, we can identify personality traits we know are likely to lead to certain outcomes, both in ourselves and in others. If those outcomes are potentially harmful, why even go down that road?

A big turn off with many potential clients is when salespeople express their values about their offerings without tying the benefits of their products back to the client's values. This might be expressed this way: "What *I really like* about this product is..." Polite clients may listen to the salesperson's opinion but aren't liable to give it any weight in decision-making unless they have the same or similar values. They couldn't care less what *others* like. They're only concerned with the benefits they'll like. Changing up how you present benefits from what you like to what they might enjoy will make a world of difference in how buyers respond to you. When they recognize that you're looking at the product or decision from their perspective, trust will grow, and they *will* value your opinion.

Another example of this is when a salesperson (or loved one) says, "You're going to love this" or "You should...." With those phrases, you are, in essence, forcing your values on the other person. Assumptions and "shoulds" are big turnoffs for most people, whether it's a business or personal situation.

A softer approach would be to say, "Some of our happiest clients love this" or "Perhaps you might consider..." Do you see and feel the difference in the approach? Practice this during your next conversation with either a client or a friend. Notice the difference in how the conversation goes.

Understanding How Decisions are Made

Buying decisions are made based on past experiences, the experiences of others, advertising, gut feelings, and hundreds of other factors that vary from client to client. None of these can be controlled by the salesperson. However, sales pros can and do work with all those factors when determining the best approach and the best product or service to present.

The important thing is to learn how to gather that information. This is done using questions to get buyers talking about their needs, perceptions, and expectations regarding possible solutions. The Champion salesperson knows that the most potent force is perception and then appeals to that force. We may have the best product at the best investment, but the truth is that the buyers will not buy it unless and until they believe that to be true. The onus is on the salesperson to help the buyer recognize that truth.

The most productive sales situations occur when knowledgeable experts ask potential buyers specific questions as they relate to their type of product. This is called qualifying. When done properly, the buyers' answers tell the salespeople what they want to own. It's then up to the sales pro to decide if what they're offering meets the criteria or needs set out by the buyers. When there's a good match, it then becomes the salesperson's obligation to share the information about their product in such a way that the buyer comes to the belief that theirs is the best solution.

Do These People Really Need Your Help?

The next step after determining values is to determine (aka qualify) the other person or people. Are they people we want to do business with or need to do business with? Can we really help them?

When it's time to get down to business, you'll want to gently change gears. Here's an example of what you might say, "You know, Mr. Johnson, when I'm not helping people get involved with (name your type of product), I'm a consumer just like you, looking for quality products at the best price. What I hope for when I'm shopping is to find someone who can help me understand and evaluate all the facts about the item I'm interested in, so I can make a wise decision. What I'm hoping for with you is to earn your trust as an expert on (name your type of product). So, let's talk about your situation and what your needs are."

That introduction was *word-smithed* to put forth a level of professionalism, not to raise defense barriers, and to engage both the emotional and logical sides of the buyer. You see, people don't buy with logic. They buy emotionally, then rationalize their decisions with logic.

Once we get people to agree to speak with us, we move into the qualification step of the sales process. Before we can qualify potential clients, we need to know what we need to know about them. Think of yourself as a doctor trying to determine an accurate diagnosis and then develop an effective prescription for wellness. Doctors want to exude confidence, so people will confide in them, right? That process is completed with a well-honed set of diagnostic tools.

Working backward from a closed sale, what information would you have needed to gain from buyers to know you have the best solution for them? When you know what those answers are, write out questions that will generate the answers. It's sort of like playing Jeopardy®. To practice this, pull up one of your sales forms.

Go through it from top to bottom and develop a simple, yet professional question that will provide each bit of information.

If your product is something of a delicate nature or something people might not be comfortable discussing with you, since they just recently met you, begin your questions with a phrase such as, "Not to be personal." "Not to be personal, Mary, but in order to do the best job of helping you get on solid footing financially, I need to ask..." Then, move into the questions you need to ask. That would be a nice lead-in for debt-relief or financial services products. You're telling them, sincerely, that you want to do your best job for them. You're alluding to the fact that they need to trust you enough to open up with the information you need in order to help them. That is a great example of using the language of sales.

Another example of how to move into qualifying is this: "Mr. & Mrs. Smith, would you be offended if I ask you a few questions that would help me to better serve your needs, save you some time, and possibly some money?" Who would say "no" to that? Not many people. Again, you're demonstrating professionalism. You're taking control of the sales process. And you're getting permission to ask the questions you need to ask.

Except for the regular purchases of daily life, the average person has difficulty making decisions about owning anything without input from others. With such a wide variety of choices of where to spend our money, decision-making can become quite complex. There are few people on the planet who have not made poor decisions. We feel safe in saying that we all want to avoid making poor decisions in the future. There's an element of fear in most decisions. This fear can be especially strong in business situations. Poor decisions can reflect poorly on us and prevent advancement.

Fear can cause indecision. And, indecision stalls sales. It's our job as professional problem-solvers to help people become confident in their knowledge of both their challenges and in the solutions we deliver.

If your company has not developed a list of information required in order to make sound recommendations of products, set aside some time to do it yourself. This would be the information you need in order to call for a decision. Any bit of information that gets overlooked could keep the sale from going through.

This is the time to ask the who, what, where, when, and why questions that focus on customer needs instead of your need to sell. Here are just a few examples of guiding questions:

1. Who made the last purchase of a product or service of this type?
2. On what criteria was their decision made?
3. Who is the primary user of the product or service? How many people in the company (or the home) are affected by the purchase?
4. What are the key concerns in making change?
5. What do you like most about your current product, and what would you change?
6. What do you want to improve?
7. What do you fear you'll lose?
8. When do you need the product or service up and running?
9. When can you begin training those involved?
10. How many people need training on this new equipment/ software?
11. Why have you considered my particular product?
12. How much product (quantity) do you think you will need?
13. How do you propose to "sell" your internal staff on this change?

14. When was the last change made, and why?
15. What colors do you like?
16. Are there any restrictions on size?

If your buyer hesitates or seems to run out of information, use prodding questions, summaries, or statements that will get them to elaborate. Some helpful phrases might sound like this:

1. "If I understand you correctly, you are saying..."
2. "Am I correct in understanding that..."
3. "The point then, is this ..."
4. "By this, do you mean..."
5. "Do you think it would help if we could provide..."
6. "Are you satisfied with your current product's ability to..."

In a sense, you need to get to your buyers' concerns about their current situations. We call the questions that bring this about *disturbing questions*. Disturbing questions are those questions that demand the buyer to confront a challenge or area of dissatisfaction about the existing product or service. Once the challenge is discovered, then you assume the role of problem-solver.

Tom

To simplify the qualification step of starting a business relationship, I teach a strategy called the N.E.A.D.S. formula. It's a way of discovering the needs of another person when it comes to your product or service. It goes like this:

N What do they have NOW?

Do they have a need for the type of product or service you represent? Do they already use your competitor's product?

Or, have they no knowledge of your type of product and need to be educated as to what it is and what it can do for them? Past history most often dictates future decisions. Unless there's been a drastic change in circumstances, most people want to purchase something like what they've owned before. Few people enjoy stepping very far outside of their comfort zones.

E What do they ENJOY most about what they have now?

What's the buyer's favorite benefit of the product they're using now that they wouldn't want to live without? Ask why that is such a great benefit to them. Your product will, at minimum, need to fulfill that same benefit. If your product is much improved over what they enjoy now, rationalizing the purchase of something better becomes easy.

A What would they ALTER or change about the product they're using now?

If we had magic wands we could wave over the product they're using now, what would they change about it? This could be anything: color, size, power, speed, functionality, anything imaginable. The answer to this question alone will tell you what they want to buy.

D Are these the people who would make buying decisions?

Do they need to consult with someone else before authorizing or making a purchase? Is there a purchasing process or a committee that needs to be consulted? Or are they the only ones who make this type of buying decision?

S The "S" in this formula stands for Solution. Your goal in qualifying is to research and analyze the other person's situation so you, with your expert knowledge, can help them find an excellent *solution* for their needs. When you express this with confidence, you'll increase the expectation and anticipation in buyers to see what you come up with.

With this formula, or a similar qualifying strategy, you're demonstrating to the buyers that you sincerely want to understand their situation, their current product and its usage, and to help them find something better. You can set the expectation that you'll be able to provide a better solution than the client is using now, or that the competition may offer. That expectation starts the rationalization process required for decisions to be made.

Re-read this segment of the book many times—at least until you have the qualification sequence down. Thousands of salespeople try to make sales each day with no idea if the people they're speaking with are even qualified to make buying decisions. They never determine if they're working with a final decision-maker. Because of this, they often end up without the information they need to present a solid solution and no sale. They waste a lot of time going nowhere. Develop the skills of strong qualifiers. It's not uncommon for them to have a closing ratio of five times greater than that of a poor qualifier.

Recognizing the Competition

When it comes to creating relationships, whether personal or professional, competition can be a tricky part of the equation. There are many different types of competition to be aware of.

- "The competition" is most often thought to be competing companies in your industry who are going after the same clients and client dollars that you are working to get.

- There's also competition among clients for your time and attention.

- On the personal side, there's competition for your interest, time, and attention by loved ones.

- In each of those areas, you have a certain level of responsibility, don't you? You're responsible for gaining the knowledge and skills to help clients and potential clients rationalize doing business with you rather than with a competitor in the industry. You're also ultimately responsible for how you use your time. Depending upon their values and emotional needs, some clients will compete for your allotted selling time. They may not be aware that they're competing with other clients when they make demands of you, but that's what happens.

It's important while discovering values and qualifying clients to determine if the creation of a new business relationship with a particularly needy client may negatively impact your ability to serve the needs of existing clients. In selling, it's not just about getting as many clients as possible. To have a successful long-term career, you need to serve each of your clients well.

Clients have value beyond the dollars they spend with you. Happy clients can easily become a source of repeat business, testimonials, and referred leads. Interactions with them require a certain amount of time and emotional effort. Be sure to weigh the value of both against the value of their transactions as you interact with them.

In personal relationships, who would someone you are creating a new relationship with be in competition with? For example, if you are a single parent, are you creating a new romantic relationship with someone who will now be competing for your time with your children? Would this new person expect you to spend time with them instead of with your other friends? Know what amount of time and effort you're willing to commit to any new relationship because every new relationship impacts all the other relationships you have.

Dealing With the Competition

It's likely that you'll encounter some tricky situations within your industry. If you are working for an insurance agency, for example, and have specialized products and services, or use internal systems that may be proprietary, sharing information with a client or professional acquaintance in the same industry could end up harming your situation at work. You can converse about the industry in general with a competitor, but you certainly don't want to share trade secrets with him or her. Why make it easy for your competitors to learn how to make things harder on you?

When you learn that an existing or potential client is considering options from the competition, set a goal to learn as much about the competition's likely offering as possible in an ethical manner. Hopefully, the competition will not be unknown to you. So, you won't be starting from scratch. Invest time in comparing the competition's product to yours. Be prepared to help your clients see the products or services in an "apples-to-apples" manner.

Unless you're in an industry that provides independent reviews of products, it's unlikely that the competition will create anything that will compare your products evenly. Be prepared to invest the time, during non-sales time, to do this work. That way you'll be ready when you hear that your clients are also considering products or solutions from another company.

Do yourself a favor and never, in print, display, or verbally, knock the competition. Instead, rise above them with the value your offering provides, and with your professional demeanor in representing your company.

When you are trying to win clients over from the competition, you want to seek out the pain points clients have about those competitors. In many cases, you will find that potential clients are not 100 percent happy with the service and attention they receive from vendors, even if they love the products. Others will be happy enough with the service they're receiving. They may even be happy enough with the product. They may have become so comfortable with the product and salesperson who serves them that they don't even try to find an improved product or consider that another sales representative might serve them better. Let's face it; we all have a goal of being comfortable—being happy with the decisions we've made. Until something better is presented to us, we may not even consider looking for it.

As sales pros, we need to use the language of sales to be somewhat disruptive. As we mentioned earlier in the book, we need to get the *attention* of buyers, build their *interest,* create *desire*, and move them to action. With the right language, we get them to open their minds to new ideas, new products, and services.

One strategy for getting buyers to open their minds to what you have to say is to talk with them about the history of their past decisions. When people are happy with what they chose, they'll want to share the details of their wise decisions with you—if you ask. Your job is to help them see that since they went out of their way to research the products, educate themselves on the benefits, and make good decisions, that the potential is there that they can do it again. Such a scenario might go like this:

You:	"Mark, are you satisfied with the benefits being provided by *Other Company?*"
Buyer:	"Yes, we have a lot of confidence in them. We haven't had any challenges, and we feel we paid a reasonable amount for the service."

Remember to be attentive to the unspoken language, as well as what is being said. Stay attuned to the speaker's body language. If he or she presses their lips together after saying this, they may just want to get this conversation over with. If they're relaxed, they may be demonstrating that they're open to hearing your version of how their needs can be handled.

You:	"How long have you been with *Other Company?*"
Buyer:	"About five years now."
You:	"And before that, were you using this type of product?"
Buyer:	"Yes. We had purchased from *Yet Another Company,* but *Other Company's* product proved to be a better choice."
You:	"And, were you involved in making the final decision to make the switch, or were others involved as well?"
Buyer:	"I was responsible for finding the best solution at the time."
You:	"That change was based on quite a bit of research and analysis, wasn't it?"
Buyer:	"Yes. It seemed like it took a lot of time, but we're happy with the results."

Now that you have the buyer talking about *how* they made their previous change, and you know they were the key decision-maker, the stage has been set. It's time to shake them out of their "comfortable" funk and open their minds to hearing what your product can do. To accomplish this, you would say, "Since you received great benefit by considering and then making a change five years ago, doesn't it make sense that, with all the changes in the marketplace, you could do it again? After all, why would you deny yourself the opportunity to repeat the situation where you received, and enjoyed, even greater benefit?"

In most cases, this strategy will earn you the right to give a presentation of your solution. Of course, you'll need to demonstrate how it differs or improves upon what they're using now. But at least you will have the chance to do so rather than being dismissed by a buyer who is "comfortable" with the competition.

Learn the pattern of that strategy. Write out the words that represent your type of sale but use the same sequence to get to the point where the buyer agrees to take the next step with you. The next phase of your job is to persuade the buyer that making the change to your product and service will bring them even more benefits and satisfaction than the competition has provided.

The goal of every strategy in this chapter has been to develop relationships by building trust. It's imperative that you create engagement with buyers, prove yourself trustworthy, and focus on what *they* want and need. When you build trust quickly and effectively, you'll earn the right to vie for their business.

4

HOW TO MAXIMIZE COMMUNICATION

"Take advantage of every opportunity to practice your communication skills so when important occasions arise, you will have the gift, the style, the sharpness, the clarity, and the emotions to affect other people."

—Jim Rohn

Our experiences create our perceptions of the world around us. And, each person has a unique experience. So, there's always a possibility that two people who agree on something will understand it completely differently. This is why it's important to learn effective communication skills and use them to our greatest advantage.

As an example, let's consider a group of people who are all from different parts of the planet. When the word "sun" is introduced into a conversation, each person may understand its definition as "the star around which the earth orbits." Yet, each may have a different emotional response to the topic of the sun.

For some, it will evoke something positive such as warmth, the knowledge that it is good for crops, "beach time," solar power, and so on. For others, it may evoke negative mental images and emotions such as sweltering, dryness, cracked earth, sunburn. Consider how all those different responses and emotions could create misunderstandings. And that's just from one word!

Do you see how amazing it is that we humans communicate effectively at all? There are so many ways to miscommunicate and to misunderstand.

The Goal of Communication

This may come as a surprise to you, but the overall goal of communication is not to be *understood*. It is to *understand* those with whom we want to communicate. When we understand how others perceive things, we can then choose the best words to communicate on a topic, the situation, or move others to action. In communication, your first goal should be to determine what's most important to others. Once you know that, you'll be able to choose the best details to highlight and the best words to use to get your point across.

You wouldn't use the same language to communicate with a four-year-old that you use with an adult. And, please don't fall into the trap of thinking you can use the same language with all adults in the business world. Again, we've all had different experiences, and will have different thoughts and emotions related to the words used.

Let's say you offer products in the technology arena. You would want to identify early in your conversation with your potential client what level of understanding they have about your type of product. Be careful here that you don't pre-judge anyone. Someone in their 60s who is tech-savvy might be offended if you spoke with them as if they don't understand technology at all. And, considering the opposite situation, not all 20-somethings are equally knowledgeable about technology. Develop a few simple questions related to your product that will give you an idea of what your starting point is as to the buyer's understanding of your type of product. Your job is to meet them at that starting point, then educate them further so they'll have enough information to make wise decisions about ownership.

Avoiding Negative Words

When you use words and phrases that people either don't understand or that generate negative emotions, you put yourself in a position of effectively swimming upstream in trying to get them to go along with you, buy your product, or join your team. Remember: Confused minds say no.

There are certain words that fall under what we call "sales jargon" that we suggest never using with potential clients. One of the most commonly used words in sales is the term "contract." What type of mental image does that term bring to your mind, especially when you picture yourself as a consumer? For most of us, it's negative. We have an image of fine print and being locked into something that requires legal action to get out of. For that reason, we recommend that salespeople stop using that term— unless your line of business requires it.

Instead, use the terms "paperwork," "agreement," or "form." Think about each of those terms for a moment. Do they bring to mind threatening images? For most people, they don't. If they do, we'll bet those images are a lot less threatening than those created by the term "contract." Do yourself a favor and eliminate the term "contract" from your vocabulary.

This advice may seem small or insignificant, but having a successful sales career is little more than creating a string of small successes. You can make major blunders and lose a sale, but we believe more sales are lost when you add up the small things that create an overall negative feeling. Making the most of the little things is nothing more than developing good habits.

Good habits are very important to a pro. The details you let slide today will likely come back to haunt you tomorrow. That is why we are teaching the basics. No living creatures get off course faster than we humans, so be sure to invest the time to get the little things right. (Did you notice the use of the term "invest" when referencing time in that last sentence? There's a different feeling between that and "spending" time, isn't there? This is just another example of how words make us feel and the pictures they create in our minds.)

What about the terms "cost" and "price?" What pictures do they create in your mind? Most people envision their hard-earned cash leaving their bank accounts. Substitute the terms "investment" or "amount" in place of "cost" or "price." When we hear the word "investment," we envision getting a return on our money, which is something positive, right? There are some products for which the term "investment" is not appropriate, such as financial services. In that field, the term "investment" is used differently. If you represent financial products, use the term "amount." Let's leave the word "cost" for the people who work in accounting.

The same idea goes for the next terms, "down payment" and "monthly payment." Most people envision "down payments" as large deposits that lock them into many smaller "monthly payments" for a considerable time period. They may see themselves receiving bills and writing checks every month. Not too positive a picture, is it? Replace those phrases with these: "initial investment" or "initial amount" and "monthly investment" or "monthly amount." Do you feel the difference? Your buyers will, too.

What about the term "buy?" There goes money out of pockets again. Let's use the term "own" instead. "Own" brings to mind images of enjoying that item or service that's being purchased, and many other positive thoughts—perhaps even showing the item with pride to friends or relatives. Pride of ownership is a very strong buying motive for some people. Learn to recognize it and use it in your sales process.

The next terms to change are "sell" and "sold." Many salespeople will tell prospective customers about how many units of their product they have sold. Or, they'll brag about having sold the same product to another customer. What are the mental images generated by those words? No one likes the idea of or the feeling derived from being "sold" anything. It sounds as if the customer didn't really have much say in the matter. Replace "sell" or "sold" with the phrases "helped them acquire" or "got them involved." Those phrases create professional images of the salesperson being helpful and the buyer being involved in the process. Buyer involvement and participation indicate a willingness to go ahead.

Another term that is over-used by salespeople is the term "deal." What does this bring to mind? Something we've always wanted, but rarely found: "a great deal." That's another phrase Hollywood has included in the script for unscrupulous characters. Top salespeople never offer deals to their clients. They offer "opportunities" or help them with "transactions."

Buyers don't raise "objections" about our products or services. They express "areas of concern." We've all seen television shows where attorneys jump up and object to something in the courtroom. Everything comes to a halt as the judge decides whether to acknowledge that objection. Rather than letting "objection" define the stalling tactics buyers employ, let's call them "concerns" or "areas of concern." Those terms are gentler on our own psyches as concerns are something that we want to address and resolve. Both "address" and "resolve" keep the sales process moving forward.

We never "pitch" our product or service to a group, committee, or buyer. We deliver professional "presentations" or engaging "demonstrations." Feel the difference? Many salespeople will use the term "pitch" when speaking to other salespeople, but please, never use it with buyers or clients.

As experts on our products and services, we don't earn "commissions." We do, however, receive "fees" for the excellent service we deliver. If hesitant or aggressive buyers ask what your commission is on a sale, reply like this: "Bill, I'll admit my company has included a fee for service in every transaction. In that way, I'm compensated for the high level of service I give to every client. You do have a high level of expectation for the service I'll deliver, don't you?"

Last, but definitely not the least important term to change is "sign." If you don't change your vocabulary with the other words covered here, please, please change this one. Never again ask a buyer to "sign" anything. What happens to us emotionally when we are asked to sign something? If you're like millions of other people on the planet, you hesitate. Warning bells go off in your head. You want to step back and make sure you're making the right decision.

From the salesperson's side of this communication, the sales process comes to a screeching halt. In some cases, the sale is killed. In others, the salesperson needs to go all the way back to re-establishing rapport, reminding the buyer how excited they were about the benefits covered in the presentation, and possibly re-addressing concerns that were raised before they can ask, again, for the sale.

Why would you put yourself through that? Just stop using the word "sign.' Instead, ask people to "approve" the paperwork, "authorize" the transaction, or "endorse" the agreement. You can even ask them to "OK" the purchase order—just be certain they add their name or initials to it and don't just put "OK" in the designated spot. If your type of sale, buyer, or demeanor is light-hearted, you can even ask the buyer for their "autograph" as you point to the appropriate spot for approval. Just stop asking people to "sign."

It may seem we're nit-picking with some of the suggestions in this chapter but think of all these little things as bricks. When you use a word that creates a negative thought or feeling, it's like handing your buyer a brick for the wall of sales resistance they're building. And, that's the opposite of what we want to have happen in sales, isn't it? We want to lower those walls, take away the bricks, or at least leave openings for windows and doors through which we can continue to communicate—moving the sales process forward.

Take an objective look at your current sales presentation and look for any words you currently use that *could* generate a negative image or emotion for your buyers. Then, work on replacing them with more positive words or at least words that are less threatening. This requires conscious effort. Then, pay attention to whether buyers respond differently to you. We think they will.

Being Assumptive Can Be a Good Thing

As a rule, it's not a good idea to be assumptive when it comes to communication. As we've already discussed, seeking clarity in every interaction is the name of the game. In sales, there are situations where you want to be assumptive, and these happen during the sales process.

At some point, you'll have enough information to know that your buyers are qualified to own your offering and that your solution truly is good for them. That's the point where being assumptive has its value. When you speak assumptively, you are speaking as if they already own the benefits of your product or service. This is a strategy with words that contribute to the overall desire of the buyer to go ahead.

This is where you substitute the word "if" as in "If we can find a solution for you today, are you in a position to go ahead with an order?" with the word "when." "When we install this new program for you, Jack, you'll be able to render those marketing reports much faster and with higher-resolution graphics." The salesperson is "assuming" the sale. The buyer is hearing that they already own it. The words create ownership thoughts. Thoughts create emotions, and emotions dictate actions.

It's okay to be assumptive when you know the decision is right for your buyer.
It's All in the Delivery

Words are readily available to all of us. Merriam Webster didn't reserve certain words and their meanings for the upper classes or the wealthy, did he? Everyone has access to the same dictionary. Everyone has the same opportunity to choose the words that make their communications memorable. When you have the choice of millions of words to establish your meaning and persuade others, why wouldn't you exert the effort required to come up with the best possible combinations?

Below are two examples of how a salesperson might approach a client. Read them through and notice how you feel about each. Then, re-read them carefully, seeking out the difference in the words that are used. Even though you cannot see these people, your mind will create images of each of them, their selling styles, and the potential each has for getting the sale.

Mrs. Worth, manager of *Just for You* hair care products, has been courting an account with a major chain of salons for months. These salons now carry Mrs. Worth's competitor's products, but the owner has agreed to hear a presentation by one of her representatives. It's now up to Mrs. Worth to choose the salesperson who will communicate most effectively and, hopefully, close the sale. She meets with several of her top salespeople and narrows her choice down to two. Which will she choose? Which would you choose?

DAWN

Mrs. Worth: "Dawn, now that I've given you the background on this client, tell me: How would you give this presentation?

Dawn: "I'd love the chance to tell Mr. Dunn how much better our products are than what he's using. I wouldn't waste any time. I'd go to his salon tomorrow morning and catch him before his day got super busy. I know I could convince him to dump what he's using now and replace that stock with ours."

Mrs. Worth:	"I like your enthusiasm, Dawn, but tell me, what's your next step?"
Dawn:	"I would simply tell Mr. Dunn what we could do for him. I'd try to get him on my side before the presentation to the rest of his decision-making team. He must be the major influencer for this decision, after all. His salon managers will do whatever he wants."
Mrs. Worth:	"You're probably right, but how would you get him on your side? What would you say."
Dawn:	"I'd tell him how much money he would save because our products are less expensive than that other brand, while they do just as good a job. He could sell them at the same amount as the competitor's products and make a greater profit."

SUE

Mrs. Worth:	"Sue, now that I've given you the background on this client, tell me how would you give this presentation?
Sue:	"I will read over all the information you have gathered so far in researching this client, so I can plan my presentation. Then, I will reach out to Mr. Dunn to find a time that's convenient for him to meet."
Mrs. Worth:	"Ok. What's next?"
Sue:	"I will ask Mr. Dunn to show me his salons—getting him to talk about his needs, his stylists' needs, and that of their clientele. Then, I will offer Mr. Dunn a trial run of

	our products and ask for permission to present the products directly to his stylists."
Mrs. Worth:	"How would you get him on your side when presenting to his stylists? What would you say?"
Sue:	"While it's important to address his financial benefits, I'll encourage Mr. Dunn to examine the condition of hair that's been treated with our products. Better results will generate happier customers who will keep coming back for both services and our products. May I have your permission to take a couple of the company models with me to the presentation when I get it scheduled?"

Of course, this was a bit of an exaggeration, so you would feel the difference in approaches between the two salespeople. It's obvious that Sue would be the better choice. She would likely make a smoother presentation because of the preparation she would do, and by putting the focus on results—not just the money. How about the different feel between the two when using "I would" versus "I will?" Did you pick up on that? Dawn's use of "I would" infers "if I got the opportunity." Sue expresses more confidence right from the beginning speaking as if she's already doing the job.

One of the biggest areas of miscommunication between people can be traced back to a few simple words that could be interpreted in more than one way. "You said…" and "Why did you say…" have been the warning shots of many a communication skirmish. One of the most important nuances of selling is to be aware of how your words impact others. It's not our goal to make you hesitant to speak at all, but to create a new awareness of how you will improve the results you're getting by the words you choose.

Recognizing Effectiveness

Knowing that we all perceive things differently based on so many factors, how do we know for sure that our communication with others is effective?

- Is it a feeling? Do you notice when you are communicating well with someone that you seem to have a better emotional connection with him or her?

- Is it achieving a result that you and the others involved agree on something?

It could be either. Sometimes it's both.

In sales, of course, the end goal is that through effective communication, you will generate a belief that your product will benefit the client so well that they agree and want to pay for it. In personal situations, the result of positive communication might be to spend more time together or to spend time together in a certain way.

Aspects of Communication

To simplify communication, it's a matter of speaking and listening. We use words to introduce ourselves to others; to open conversations; to ask questions and gather information; to deliver information and get feedback; to comment or engage with others, and to make requests. In the world of selling, the most important requests are closing questions, also known as asking for the business. We will cover them in detail in a later chapter.

When it comes to listening, it's just as important to pay attention to the words used by the other parties as it is to watch what you say. Don't just listen to what they say. Listen to how they say it. There's that adage, "It's not what you say that matters. It's how you say it." We don't believe that one. In effective communication, both matter!

Prove this to yourself. In your next conversation, whether personal or in business, really pay attention to the words used by the other party or parties. Then, invest a few minutes in considering whether those words could have different meanings than what you initially understood. If you fear a miscommunication has occurred, address it immediately. Request clarification from the other parties as simple as saying, "If I understand you correctly," and then stating a fact or a need you believe the buyer has indicated is important.

Here's another little test for you to try. Pay attention to the amount of time during your next conversation that you are speaking versus listening to the other person. If you realize that you are doing most of the talking, consider why that is. If you really want to become more knowledgeable about the people you are having conversations with, whether personal or professional, you must focus on listening as much as possible, and you create listening opportunities by asking questions. Being good listeners is how introverts do well in sales. They are just fine with keeping the limelight on the other party or parties to the sales conversation by encouraging them to elaborate. They are interest*ed* rather than trying to be stereotypical interest*ing* extroverted salespeople.

Sadly, there's a great gap in the time spent communicating and the time spent learning to communicate. On average, adults spend

40 percent of their time listening to others, yet only about one year of formal education is spent learning *how to listen*. Thirty-five percent of our time is spent talking—something we only spend about two years learning. Sixteen percent of our time is spent reading, which we think you'll agree is a critical skill. And, we spent six to eight years learning how to do it well. We spend about nine percent of our time writing—hopefully, writing effective communications—and up to twelve years learning how to do it. Do you see the discrepancy? Our education system focuses more on writing rather than on where most of our communications occur: Listening and Talking.

Effective listening isn't taught as an important skill other than elementary school children being told *to* listen—but not taught *how to* listen. You may have heard the term "active listener" in a communications class or training session. The basics include giving the speaker your undivided attention. (We will cover distractions in a minute.) It's polite to acknowledge what the speaker is saying through body language, such as making eye contact, nodding, or smiling when appropriate. Taking notes is a great way of showing that you're listening.

In sales situations, it's wise to ask permission to take notes or mention that you want to take notes (showing how important it is to you to remember details). Be prepared to also give feedback on what's been said, and if you need additional information, be willing to encourage others to tell you more.

Being a good listener means that you're listening to understand. If the other person says anything that isn't clear, you will want to get clarification before you speak with them about that topic or benefit. Doing so can be as simple as saying, "Joe, a moment ago you mentioned _____. Would you mind clarifying what you mean by that? I want to be clear, so I don't waste your time by suggesting a solution that doesn't meet your needs." As a general rule, people like being helpful. Don't be afraid to ask for help so you can do your job as best as you possibly can. When you ask a question about something specific your buyer said, it demonstrates to them that you were truly listening—another way to build trust.

The Planned Pause

When you are asked a question by a customer, take a moment to consider it before answering. Even if you have the answer at the tip of your tongue, it's often best to pause a moment to consider why they may be asking the question. What else might they have in the backs of their minds? Jumping on the question to give a quick answer doesn't always come across properly. While you may be thinking that they'll be impressed with your quick knowledge, they may be thinking you must have heard this question before or that your answer is too slick, too prepared. By pausing a moment, the buyer will get the impression that you're giving careful consideration to your answer. Depending upon the question, this could increase their perception of your level of competency as a representative of this product or service.

Always remember this: There is no such thing as a dumb question from a buyer. As a matter of fact, what they might think of as a dumb question could mean an easy sale because they want it, can't think of an objection, but feel they should ask something. Let's look at the following example. The salesperson has just shown Mr. Black a home that meets all his needs, and after successfully overcoming the few concerns Mr. Black has, the salesperson attempts to consummate the sale.

Salesperson:	"Mr. Black, here is the list of things you said you wanted in a home. I think we both agree this home has everything you mentioned, doesn't it?"
Mr. Black:	"Well, yes, I guess so. Uh, how many times have you shown this house, anyway?"

The best way to address a question that seems irrelevant or unimportant is to first recognize it for what it is—a stall, a question that is asked because the customer doesn't know what else to do to allow himself a breather. The customer feels he or she should ask some questions but doesn't really know what to ask. The salesperson could simply choose to focus on the part of Mr. Black's response that is pertinent to the sale. He has as much as said this house meets all his requirements. Such as:

> Salesperson: "It's been shown to other buyers, but all home buyers are different and have different needs. I'm glad you agree that this home has the features you are looking for. Is being in your new home by Christmas still your goal?"

If Mr. Black responds with another seemingly unimportant question, then the salesperson will need to determine what is making Mr. Black uncomfortable about going ahead with his purchase of the home. What is the real objection? Obviously, it is not how many times the home has been shown. So, what is it?

It is often that most people don't want to be considered an easy sale. When the solution you've presented is more ideal than the client anticipated, or the decision is easier than they're used to, it may throw them off and cause them to stall and second-think themselves. When this happens, it's okay to brag a little, if you do it correctly.

Bring up the point that you know you may have thrown them with such a great solution—basically presenting a "no-brainer" decision. Then use what is called the "Most Productive Thing" close. With this close, you simply point out that you understand their days are filled with decisions and other important matters. Point out that by making this decision in a timely manner not only gets the solution put in motion but gets them back to their other important work. This is a way of encouraging the sale without rushing the client.

Barriers to Communication

Whether we like it or not, we all have a bit of the "know it all" in us. And that trait is the cause of many of our communication issues. We *think* we understand. We *think* we know what the other person is going to say. That "know-it-all-it is" is what we call a barrier to communication. It keeps us from listening to understand. When we listen with all our senses and no expectations of what we'll hear, communication improves.

Other barriers to communication are the simple distractions of everyday life. Phones are ringing, text messages are beeping or vibrating in, cars and trucks drive by, horns honk, emergency vehicles scream, planes fly over, elevators ding, other people interrupt, things are dropped, spilled, or misplaced. And, most importantly, the conversation may not be as important to the other parties as it is to you. They may simply be distracted by the other things on their minds. That last distraction occurs often in sales situations. You, the salesperson, are just one cog in the wheel of their business day.

One of the worst barriers to communication is more personal. Are you tired? Not on top of your game? Do you put proper fuel into your body, so it and your mind are running, like many, on caffeine and sugar? Believe it or not, how our bodies function impacts our ability to communicate well.

The former president of the *American Society for Training and Development*, Lisa J. Downs, found that there is a long list of traits that make people poor listeners. Here are the traits that she noted:

1. Daydreaming (thinking about unrelated topics when someone is speaking)
2. Debating (having an inner argument about what is being said)
3. Judging (letting negative views influence you)
4. Problem-solving (yearning to give unasked-for advice)
5. Pseudo-listening (pretending to be a good listener)
6. Rehearsing (planning what you want to say next)
7. Stage hogging (redirecting the conversation to suit your own goals)
8. Ambushing (gathering information to use against the other person)
9. Selective listening (only responding to the parts of the conversation that interest you)
10. Defensive listening (taking everything personally)
11. Avoidant listening (blocking out what you don't want to hear)

How many of these poor listening references apply to you? As a master external communicator who truly understands the value of selling yourself, your ideas, your influence, and creating certain emotions, you must be able to overcome these bad listening habits.

Think of it this way. When you are using *internal* communication, you are delivering a monologue to yourself where only your opinion matters. In *external* communication with others, everyone's opinion matters.

This not only changes the dynamic considerably but requires all your listening skills to maximize the value of the communication. Remember, when you are speaking, you aren't learning anything new. You're only saying what you already know. When you are listening, you are learning about someone else's wants, needs, desires, goals, and dreams. This doesn't mean it should be the other person delivering a monologue but imagine how much more effective you will be when you clearly understand where the person or people you are communicating with are coming from. Understanding those opinions is critical to the success of your sales process.

Active Questioning

The best plan when entering a conversation with someone you don't know very well—or at all, for that matter—is to consider it as an opportunity to learn. Not many people are skilled at asking "learning" questions in a conversation because they don't practice this very often. In fact, they don't practice listening very often, either. Remember, you must focus on the key outcomes you want the conversation to have prior to starting it, or there is no way to know where to go with it. Your goal is to learn about someone's personal or professional history, which can predict future actions. Your best chance to do so is by asking questions.

When you want to learn the most you can about another person, employ what we call "active questioning and learning" with the intent to utilize the information to better understand that person and his or her goals. This will start with you having a goal in mind to learn at least three to five key things that the other person is interested in from his or her personal and professional life.

This will take practice, of course, but imagine how quickly you can master this skill if you start doing this every time you meet someone new. The object here is not to make every new conversation an inquisition, mind you, but if you want to really learn about someone, you have to ask and listen more than you want to talk about yourself and your personal and professional past. If you find yourself talking too much, even the conversation process out by asking a question or multiple questions. It is important to ask questions that won't offend, of course, but don't be afraid to ask questions that require some thought versus questions that you think you may already know the answer to.

Here are some examples, both business-related and personal, that will help you when starting to use this technique of active questioning and learning:

"If money wasn't an issue, how would you invest your time?"
"If money wasn't an issue, what would be your ideal solution to this challenge?"
"What was the most fun job you ever had?"
"How do you like your position here at (name of company)?"
"If you could live any place in the world, where would that be?"
"What accomplishments are you most proud of in your career/life?"
"What are some of the things that you were sure you were going to hate and ended up doing anyway and loving as a result?"
"What has surprised you most in your position as (position title)?"

As you read these questions, what do you notice about them? They all require an answer other than yes or no, so you know they are open-ended questions. The reason you want to ask these types of questions when first meeting people is because you will learn quickly how much they do or don't like sharing information about themselves. If you only ask "yes" or "no" questions or closed-ended questions, you will still learn something, but nowhere near as much. With open-ended questions like these, not only will you learn, but something else will happen. You will instantly get a feeling about how important the conversation is.

Think about situations where you thought you were having a great conversation, talking most of the time about yourself, of course, only to learn the next time you saw the person that he or she didn't even remember your name because there was no connection. This happens because most people are more interested in sharing what is important to them than learning what is important to others, again through active questioning and learning.

What if the person doesn't respond well to questions or is shy and shows discomfort about answering your questions? This doesn't make him or her a bad person, of course, but it does alert you to the fact that it may take a while to get to know them. Is that a good thing or a bad thing? It's up to you to decide that, but again, now you have a better idea of what is to come with this person. In a personal relationship, this could affect the amount of time it takes for the relationship to grow.

Maybe you are the one who is not used to sharing much at the beginning of a relationship and are waiting for someone else to get the ball rolling. This technique of active questioning and learning allows you to ask questions and learn without having to share unless you want to or until the other person asks you to.

Become a good questioner, so you can more easily learn about others. And, be prepared with answers of your own to share if and when you feel comfortable doing so. This will make others more comfortable with you because it won't seem that the conversation is one-sided.

What we've listed here are just a small number of the many questions that you could ask someone to create an opportunity to use active questioning and learning. No matter who the conversation is with, these questions will give you insight into the type of person you are speaking with, which can only help you to better assess what the future may hold. Whether a personal or professional relationship may be ahead, one thing is for sure, and that is you will gain some potentially valuable information. The most important thing is that you are learning about that person and their motivations.

Uncovering other people's motivations may cause you to reconsider pursuing a business relationship. In business, you want to pay attention to how they speak about their current vendors. Do they state facts about how the relationship is going? Or, are they inserting derogatory remarks? If they display a hostile attitude toward their current vendor, how will they treat you?

Avoid Questions that Allow One-Word Answers

A no answer only gets you one piece of information. The more you can get your customers to say, the better your chances are to get information you can use to help them.

Try to make a game with your friends or family of questions that can't be answered by a yes or no. In fact, it often helps to turn your sales drills and practice into games. It has been said that all life is a game with rules and costs. The rules aren't always easy to follow, and the costs aren't always pleasing, but the winners accept the challenges and reap the rewards. Remind yourself that no one will be able to escape an occasional failure when they accept challenges.

Discovery through questions allows you to learn from others as much or more than they learn from you so you can walk away from almost any conversation or exchange with more information than you started with. This doesn't mean simply asking a question, sort of or half-listening with little interest, and then just saying what you were going to say anyway. This means legitimately listening to both hear and to understand before expecting someone to listen to you. Imagine what you could learn from others if this was your approach to every conversation.

Obviously, there are times when you are giving instruction or explaining something in which questions may not be appropriate. In many cases, however, we know that people make assumptions about what they think someone is going to say before they even finish a sentence, cut them off, and start to provide an answer that doesn't even fit the situation. Has that ever happened to you? Have you ever done that to someone else and then realized after when they corrected what you thought they were saying? It happens to all of us from time to time, but it doesn't have to if you follow a couple of simple keys each time you are having a conversation, whether sales-related or not.

First, take the time to better understand the person or people you are communicating with before expecting them to understand you. We have all heard of this concept, but rarely do we see people practice it. Why, you might ask? Primarily because most people are thinking about what they want to say in a communication before they are thinking about what they might hear from someone else. We understand, but sometimes forget or don't necessarily relate to the fact that we have one mouth and two ears, which could mean we should listen twice as much as we talk, right?

Do you follow that practice in your daily life, or do you find yourself talking or looking to share your point of view twice as much as you listen or consider something others are saying? Do you find yourself wanting to jump in before someone has finished speaking because you are certain you know what he or she is going to say? We all do these things from time to time, but again, there are simple ways to avoid this becoming a regular occurrence for you. Here is a way for you to test yourself on this. In your next conversation, pay attention consciously, if you can, to what percentage of the time you are talking versus listening.

If the percentage is higher than 50 percent, you know you are probably talking too much and not listening enough. If the percentage is under 50 percent and that is a regular occurrence, the likelihood is that you are learning more about the person or people you are having a conversation with. Remember, if you are talking, you can't be learning, right? The more you learn about others in your communications, the more likely you are to understand what is important to them, and the better your communication is likely to be in the future. Use these keys and steps to continue to practice listening and understanding more about others without feeling like you have to talk more than you need to and watch how much better your conversations go.

The fact is we are always selling our ideas and our influence even in casual conversation because we want people to value what we have to say. The only challenge is that when we communicate with the mindset that what we have to say is most important, we end up staying the same while those who are focused on learning from others end up learning.

5

EFFECTIVE COMMUNICATION WITH THE WRITTEN WORD

"Writing isn't letters on paper. It's communication. It's memory."

—Isaac Marion

If you've ever penned a letter, put it in an envelope, added postage, and mailed it to someone who would not receive it for several days or even longer, today's environment of text, email, and communication through social media platforms is quite a change. We have the capability of sending messages to others across the planet in literally seconds. That's also how quickly we can create chaos with the written word.

We find it interesting in the letters shown in documentaries, such as Ken Burns' *The Civil War,* how few cross outs or corrections were made. Time moved more slowly then. Perhaps people gave more thought to what they wanted to say and how they wanted to express themselves. Investing time in thought before writing is an essential key to success even today when using the language of sales.

For most, the days of writing physical letters and mailing them are over. Yet, the importance of getting the written word right has intensified. It's easy to have the written word misinterpreted when communication is made in 280 characters or fewer and when we rely on auto-correct rather than carefully checking our own work.

When you think of your daily routine and the people you encounter, what is the most common factor? Communication via mobile phones has become prevalent. Businesses of all sizes can be run from the palms of our hands. Mobile phones are readily accessible and easily utilized by everyone from age two to 102. Even those who are homeless often have mobile phones with which to communicate.

All around us, people are engaging in more screen time than ever. They're looking at their phones, tablets, laptops, or desktop computers and are engaged in some sort of communication—most likely via the written word with text, email, and social media being most prevalent. This indicates that developing our communication skills is more important than ever before.

As we covered in chapter 4, it's critical that we understand the impact our words have on others. This is especially true with written words. When communicating via writing, we don't have the in-person benefit of relying on voice inflection and body language to assist with the meaning of our words. The other parties can't see our warm smiles or non-confrontational postures. Hence the popularity of emojis or emoticons to assist with the nonverbal aspect of communication via text. While many people see no challenge with using emojis, others find them unprofessional or even confusing. You must know your audience and make choices about the use of them and text shortcuts accordingly.

This is your opportunity to separate yourself from the majority and go about your personal and professional life in a way that gives you the greatest return available to you. You can separate yourself from the pack by being great at what everyone else is doing halfway. Open yourself up to the art of communicating with the written word in a way that people will remember. With the hustle and bustle of life that we face daily, you may not believe that you have the time to go out of your way to be extremely different from others when it comes to communicating, but that's exactly why to do it. The recipients of your communications will recognize and appreciate your efforts.

A perfect example of this is the handwritten thank you note. Hopefully, you've been the recipient of one. It was probably the first item you opened in your pile of mail that day. Most people open "personal" mail before business mail or junk mail. That's the value of the handwritten note. When you want to get someone's attention, send one! Handwritten notes are not only more likely to get opened first, but to be saved and read more than once. In your personal life, a handwritten note demonstrates sincerity and thoughtfulness. It does the same in a business setting, but it also helps you to stand out as being different—as being dedicated to serving your clients well. Expressing appreciation to those in your life, whether for business or personal reasons, is a wonderful habit to develop.

When you send a text, then have to add to it because the text software auto-corrected your words to mean something else, you've done double the work. And, you may have caused confusion in the mind of the receiving party. When crafting any message, slow yourself down a bit. Focus on what result you expect the message to create. Then, write your message. Read it to yourself, preferably out loud, before hitting send. Yes, this may slow you down, but it may also eliminate miscommunication with others, and there's a high value on that.

Ten Tips for Creating Excellent Written Communication

We all want to be remembered for the exceptional things we do whenever possible, don't we? Here are ten important tips for creating excellent written communications:

Check your spelling before you send a written communication. Misspellings create a lack of confidence in the mind of the recipient. If you have a lot of misspelled words, recipients may question your intelligence. You may be the pre-eminent expert in your field but just not good at spelling. Rely on the tools that are available to you. By correcting spelling errors, you demonstrate professionalism, attention to detail, and competence. It's especially important to spell the recipient's name and business name correctly. When in doubt, invest the minute or two it will take to verify the information.

Pay attention to the words and phrases you use in your written communication—this is so you have a lower chance of offending the person or group you are communicating with. Ask yourself if any of the words you've used have more than one meaning or could be misconstrued. Consider reading the message out loud to yourself to ensure your message is clear.

Keep it professional. Avoid using slang, industry, or sales jargon unless you know for certain that the other party is familiar with those terms. When in doubt, wait to see if your potential client uses jargon before using it yourself.

Be honest and sincere in your written communications. Remember that this communication can, and many times will, be saved and might be forwarded to higher-ups at your company. Keeping everything honest and sincere is a must.

Don't be too wordy—if you have a specific message you want to deliver, keep it clear and concise. Unless you are communicating with a list or agenda of topics, keep each message to a single topic. This makes it easier for the other party to send you a quick reply. Also, when covering a single topic in an email, be sure to put that topic in the subject line. If the subject of replies changes, change the subject line, too. This practice makes it easier for all involved to track conversations on the various topics.

Create value in your written communication. Ensure that you're adding to the other person's knowledge or enhancing your relationship with them by the words you use.

Write from the heart. Let others know how much you care about them when writing simply by being kind. Always express gratitude for the relationship or the actions of the other party in your messages.

Read your communications at least once before sending them. The last thing you want to do is to have grammatical errors, missing or incorrect words, improper context, or anything that doesn't make sense in your written communication. There are many words that are spelled the same but have different meanings, such as *content, discount, project,* and *extract,* to name a few.

Don't be afraid to show your personality and character in your written communications so others can tell that you are someone they want to be involved with both personally and professionally.

Enjoy the journey of enhancing your written communication skills. Pay attention to the messages you receive and how they make you feel. With those messages that make you feel good or entice you to take action,n invest a little time analyzing the words used to see if you might use them effectively, too.

No matter what type of communication you are engaged in, you are attempting to deliver a message that you believe is important, whether personally or professionally, that will reflect who you are as a person. That is why we encourage you to make every thought and every word count. This is especially true in written communication because people can read your message over and over, forward it and share it with others, and, most importantly, use it to make decisions about future relationships. That one reason alone should have you focusing a considerable amount of energy to ensure that you are not just competent in the area of written communication, but exceptional.

How Good are You... Really?

Be honest with yourself about how strong your writing skills are. If you have doubts about the words you use, take advantage of the technology solutions available to you. Most writing programs include options for reviewing spelling and grammar in the documents you create. An online thesaurus can help you avoid overusing descriptive terms. Never hesitate to run checks on your writing. But don't assume the software will get it right every time. You may use specific words and phrases for specific purposes. Take time to consider each change the software recommends. Don't just automatically assume it's correct for your meaning. Granted, this takes a little extra effort on your part, but it's worth it when you can eliminate or minimize the risk of being misunderstood.

Written communication continues to evolve with new platforms and venues for people to exchange information. The one thing that hasn't changed is that everything you write can be saved, shared, and re-read. With that in mind, make sure you are at your best in every written communication. Remember that the focus in all your communication, whether it is internal or external, verbal or nonverbal, even written, is to deliver a message.

Idiosyncrasies of Written Communication

Time marches on. Methods of communication evolve. We must evolve with them to remain relevant and be perceived as being "on top of our game." People who were born in the 20th Century were raised in an environment where keyboarding skills were vital, fax machines were prevalent, and long-distance calls were well-planned because they were costly. Those born in the 21st Century were raised in a "texting" and social media environment where net lingo, emojis, and speed became the norm. "Unlimited text and talk" became the slogans of nearly every mobile phone provider, and nearly everyone over the age of 10 had a mobile phone.

Just because you know shortcuts doesn't mean you should always use them. Just because communication mediums are evolving doesn't mean you should always switch to them either. Being professional means that you use the most appropriate medium *for each client*—in the most appropriate way.

If the people you're communicating with prefer to do so via text and they send you CYE (Check Your Email), IHU (I Hear

You), IDK (I Don't Know), or other shortcuts in their messages, it will be important to both understand and properly use those phrases. It's their lingo. You must become multi-lingual—even when the language is slang—to communicate effectively with buyers and clients. The closer you can come to using the language of others, the better. People don't buy what you're selling because they understand what you're offering. They buy from you when they feel they are understood. And you help them see that you understand them by using their language.

Do not use emojis unless you know the current meaning of them and know that the people you're communicating with use them, too. The meaning of emojis can change even faster than technology changes. Never risk sending yesterday's image of a daisy when today it could be a symbol of something controversial.

Also, remember the Miranda warning when posting any communication online—this includes email. "Anything you 'say' can and will be used against you...." This is why it pays to double- and triple-check your written words before emailing, texting, or posting. The other party or parties have proof of what you "said."

We already referred to this in chapter 4, but using the incorrect word puts a dent in your credibility. Some of the most common include:

"To," and "Too"
"Their," "They're" and "There"
"Accept" and "Except"
"Affect" and "Effect"
"Farther" and "Further"
"Fewer" and "Less"
"Than" and "Then"

The rule of thumb here is always, "When in doubt, look it up." When you look up the answer and use the words correctly, you'll always look better in the eyes of the reader. And, bonus, you'll likely remember the correct use for next time—thus saving time in the future.

Professionalism and courtesy always come first, whether in oral or written communications. When writing messages, it's even more important to go for clarity because you may not get a chance later to clarify points that are misunderstood. You may lose the opportunity to create a business relationship.

6

THE POWER OF NONVERBAL COMMUNICATION

"Nonverbal communication forms a social
language that is in many ways richer
and more fundamental than our words."
—Leonard Mlodinow

We see it in nature all the time: postures, posing, stances that "speak" volumes in creatures who cannot use words. We can sense by its stance when a dog is wary of our approach. We recognize when our cats are hunting prey—even if they're just crickets or flies. Their bodies help us understand what's going on in their minds. So, why would we ignore what's being communicated nonverbally with our fellow human beings? Just because we humans can use words to communicate doesn't mean our bodies aren't speaking, too.

It's not only our bodily movements that speak but how we choose to present ourselves visually. Dressing for success has been a popular concept for decades. Our grooming and choice of clothing "speaks" volumes about us. Even though the "uniform" for business has become less formal with high performers such as Steve Jobs, Richard Branson, and Mark Zuckerberg choosing more relaxed styles of clothing over suits, our personal choices make certain impressions, and it's important to put forth the impression you want with each type of client.

In sales, how we carry ourselves can make the difference between having an average career and being a top performer. In a study of 10,000 people who made buying decisions, conducted by U.C.L.A., each person was asked what their initial impressions were of someone they later said "yes" to. Seven percent said the person had good knowledge of the topic, product, or service. Thirty-eight percent said the person had good voice quality—they sounded confident and intelligent. And 55 percent said the person walked with an air of confidence and self-assurance.

That "air of confidence" is best demonstrated with posture. Pay attention to yours. Do you stand and walk with your shoulders slumped? Or do you hold them slightly back to generate a more erect stance? What are your arms doing while you walk or stand? Are they limply hanging by your sides? Or, do they project energy by actively moving and gesturing?

Body language is a science, and the study of it can be quite fascinating. We highly recommend taking at least a mini-course in it to understand both sides of the body-language conversation: 1) What others are saying with their bodies; and 2) How to speak well with your own body.

Looking Like an Expert

Our recommendation when it comes to dress and grooming is to dress like the person your clients or potential clients go to for advice. After all, your goal as a sales professional is to demonstrate a certain level of expertise when it comes to your industry and product. It's also important not to dress too dramatically different from those clients.

For example, if you sell construction equipment and your decision-makers wear jeans and company polo shirts, showing up to a meeting in a high-end suit might be off-putting. If you're meeting with potential investors for your business, the suit might be very appropriate.

As you dress each morning, ask yourself, "What impression do I want to put out there today with the people I'll meet?" Then, dress accordingly. When in doubt about how to portray yourself visually, invest in a consultation with a personal shopper or image consultant. It can be one of the best investments you'll ever make outside of your career-specific education.

Your Surroundings

If most of your business communications are via online video conferencing, pay extra attention to your grooming—hairstyle, makeup, jewelry, manicures—anything that might be seen on screen. Also, pay attention to what others see in the background during video conferencing. Take a lesson from professional set designers and directors and "view the scene." Nothing should be in the background unless it adds to your professional image. Dead plants? Live plants that appear as if they're growing out of the top of your head? A messy bulletin board? Notice everything they will see. What else is in the picture? You want the other parties' focus on you and your message, not your background.

When meeting others in person, don't stop at considering what you're wearing. Is there a chance your potential client might see you drive up to your meeting? Is the exterior of your vehicle in good condition... and clean? What about anything you bring with you? A briefcase? Laptop or tablet? Presentation materials? Samples? EVERYTHING tells a story about you! Look at everything through the eyes of your potential client. They are judging everything about you, consciously or not. Don't let some minor thing that you have control over become a deterrent to doing business.

Who is Approachable?

Imagine standing in front of someone with whom you are having a conversation, and you notice that his or her body does not seem to agree with the words that are being said. Has that ever happened to you? If you pay attention to more than the words that are being said in your next in-person communication, you will notice how large a role nonverbal communication plays in our conversations. In fact, management consultant Peter Drucker noted that "The most interesting thing in communication is hearing what isn't said."

What is really interesting to note about communication with others is that when you first meet someone, whether in a social or business setting, you might actually end up having a higher percentage of nonverbal communication than you have verbal communication. Consider this example of how that might play out for you. Let's say you are at a social or business event, and you are talking to friends or colleagues and suddenly notice someone whom you have seen before but don't personally know. Would you walk up to that person and just strike up a conversation without any introduction? It depends.

If that person is surrounded by others whom you don't know, you may hesitate or ask those you do know if they can make introductions. If the person is alone, you'll consciously (or subconsciously) sense whether they're approachable. Are they standing half-turned as if they're ready to make a quick exit? Are their arms crossed or open? Are they confidently glancing around the room for others with whom to connect? Or are they looking at objects instead of people? All these things and more are easily recognized and interpreted by most adults, which helps us determine our courses of action. The trick is to make that interpretation conscious.

Facial Expressions

There are 43 muscles in the human face. They all contribute to a variety of expressions. When we make facial expressions, we're essentially transmitting a packet of information that can be received, read, and interpreted by others. By contracting or expanding our facial muscles in varying degrees and combinations, we can produce thousands of different messages that provide cues to our overall emotional state, our mental well-being, our personality and mood, our physical health, our credibility, and whether we view others as being credible. And that's just the tip of the iceberg of emotions we can express with those facial muscles.

Just think about all the ways we speak with our eyes. We send different messages by making direct eye contact, avoiding eye contact, rolling our eyes, squinting, staring, and so on. In business communications, it's important to establish rapport by making direct eye contact with everyone you meet and smiling a genuine smile that shows in your eyes.

The Handshake

What is the first thing you are likely to do when introducing yourself? Depending on your culture and how you were raised, you might start by extending your hand to shake the other person's hand. The question is, how would that handshake go? Allan Pease, an Honorary Professor of Psychology at ULIM International University, believes that the first handshake often decides what you think about other people.

Specifically, Pease notes that there are three basic types of handshakes that you are likely to encounter when first meeting someone. The first is when you extend your arm and hand straight out with your fingers pointing straight toward the individual you are meeting. The second would be where your hand is over the hand or more on top of the other person's hand. The third would be where your hand is under the hand or more underneath the other person's hand. What differences come to your mind when you think of these three different handshakes?

According to Pease, the straightforward handshake declares that you are both on neutral or even ground. The over-handed handshake declares that the person with that hand position is the dominant party. The under-handed handshake declares that the person with that hand position is the submissive party. Have you ever consciously chosen one of these hand positions? This is a prime example of how nonverbal communication can set the tone for the conversation that follows even without a single word being exchanged.

There are a number of other things to consider when it comes to the handshake and greeting. The first is the grip pressure. You obviously don't want to put your hand out with the intention of it being what's referred to as a "dead fish," which is an extremely passive example. On the other hand, you don't want to use too much pressure and potentially injure the person whose hand you are shaking, which is an extremely aggressive example. Somewhere between the two is recommended so you and the person whose hand you are shaking are both comfortable.

Consider what other gestures you might use to make others feel as comfortable as possible. This might include looking at their eyes when shaking hands. This is a sign of respect and will promote that person looking at your eyes. This can be especially important when a man is shaking hands with a woman. The last thing you want someone to think when you are greeting him or her is that your eyes are wandering, which could be construed as rude on a personal level or unprofessional on a business level. In either case, you always want to be regarded as polite and professional by the people you meet.

In some cases, where the meeting is male to male, you might add a pat on the elbow or shoulder when greeting with a hand-shake. This is a friendly gesture that can relax tension, assuming you do this in a way that is not too aggressive. In cases where it is female to female, you might see the two exchange a hug and/ or hold the hand of the other for a little longer than you typically see with males. This is, of course, different from person to person but allows a little bit of flexibility from trying to do the exact same thing every time with every person you meet.

In any case, when you are meeting and greeting someone, it is important that you keep the greeting more neutral than over the top in any direction. This establishes a greeting in a positive manner. As a side note here, be aware that not everyone is comfortable shaking hands. If your buyers are primarily elderly, there's a chance they may have arthritis or another ailment that causes them to hesitate to shake hands. It's not a sign that they don't like you. Again, in sales, your goal is always to make the other parties feel comfortable. Increasing your awareness and sensitivity to such matters will go a long way toward your success.

Group Presentations

Group presentations can be tricky. Each person in the group may have a different interpretation of your body language. It will be important to use the most neutral positioning until you can observe how they're responding to you. Pease notes that when you are presenting information and your hands are facing up, you are more likely to get buy-in from people. That's because you're nonverbally asking for approval with that gesture. It's as if you are opening up to them by having your hands up and gesturing in a fashion that implies everything you are asking of them is optional. Thus, they see what you are saying as non-threatening.

When you are speaking to a group and your hands are faced down the entire time, a completely different message comes across. This declares that you are instructing more than asking. This can build up the defenses of your listeners as they now feel like you are almost telling them what to do as opposed to sharing an idea or option with them. This can cause people to feel less comfortable with following the idea or option based on their belief that you are attempting to dominate the situation through nonverbal communication.

Another example is when you are speaking to a group and essentially pointing with one finger while speaking. This declares that you are directing. This use of body language is not typically received in a positive way. It can be interpreted that you are stating, nonverbally, that you are in charge and that your audience had better listen to you. Rather than pointing with a finger, soften your intention by using a pen or another type of pointer to direct their attention or make a point.

Another key point in group presentations is to pay attention to where everyone sits. The real final decision-maker usually takes up a position of importance, for example, at the head of a table. Some decision-makers use a tactic where they purposely choose not to take that position, but the way others react to that person will usually tell you who they are. Again, this is done through observation of the body language of each member of the group.

Consider this example the next time you are speaking to someone. Imagine you are asking someone a closed-ended question that you think you know the answer to (usually either "yes" or "no"). Now imagine that the person is answering yes, which is the opposite of what you expected, but slowly shaking his or her head no. Which would you be more likely to believe? The verbal answer "yes" or the headshaking "no?" Going back to the percentages in that U.C.L.A. study, you might be more likely to believe the body language. If that's the case, your job of persuading isn't over. You'll want to ask more questions to confirm the positive answer rather than assume and have the sale fall through later.

In fact, during every communication with others, you'll want to watch for various body language signs. Here are just a few to be aware of:

LEANING FORWARD OR BACK. When we are especially interested in something, we tend to lean forward, as if not to miss any details. When we have hesitation about what we're seeing or hearing, we tend to lean back. When a potential client leans forward, keep going, or elaborate on the point just prior to that action. When they lean backward, slow down, perhaps even pause and ask a question about the point just covered. It could be that they need clarification.

GLANCING AWAY OR DOWN. A similar action would be to remove eyeglasses or set a pen down. Most often, this indicates a need or desire to pause, to let things sink in, to evaluate. It can also mean that the other person doesn't like something you've said. When you see this, pause. Don't rush to speak. Allow the other person to have "a moment." Then, ask how they're feeling about all of this so far. Give them space to ask questions about what's been covered so far rather than moving forward on your next point. It may even help to deliver a summary or brief recap at this point in the presentation.

LOOKING INTENTLY AT YOU. This is a sign of interest. They may also tilt their heads slightly, touch their chins, or the side of the face. When you realize that you have their full attention, keep going on the path you're on. Keep the sales process moving forward.

LACK OF EYE CONTACT OR HAND COVERING MOUTH WHEN SPEAKING. When someone won't make good eye contact with you, it's likely they don't trust what you're saying. Another consideration is that they may lack confidence in their ability to evaluate your offering and make a wise decision. This person will likely stall the decision-making process unless you can help them feel confident with the knowledge you're imparting.

PULLS ON EAR. This is a common way of indicating they want to break into the conversation. Their thoughts are elsewhere, or they are trying to process or understand something that's been said. When you see this happen, pause and ask if there's a question or if you need to clarify something.

HOLDS HANDS TOGETHER WITH FINGERTIPS TOUCHING AND POINTED UPWARDS. This is an indication of high self-confidence. If you're approaching a moment of decision, this is likely a positive sign. If you see this at the beginning of your presentation, it's a sign that the person feels superior to you. Let them. Compliment them. Acknowledge their authority and express sincere appreciation for their time. This is when you display your attitude of servitude.

SQUIRMING, PLAYING WITH A PEN OR OTHER SMALL ITEM. These indicate all sorts of distractions in the minds of the doers. They may also be feeling some pressure about making a decision. You may need to take a break in your presentation or move to a point where you require physical involvement by the other party. Or, you may need to alter the pace of your presentation, such as speeding up to hold their attention.

Although these body language cues are general, when you're aware of them, you can depend on them to alert you to potential challenges during your buyer or client contacts. When you study body language on a deeper level, you'll garner even more information of value to you in all communications.

It's important to be attuned to these nonverbal cues in order to ensure that you are receiving the most accurate message possible as opposed to the message that the other person may be intentionally trying to deliver. This doesn't mean that you need to go around being paranoid or not ever trust that someone is telling you the truth, but it does beg the question how much more could you learn about someone if you focused on the nonverbal messages at least as much if not more than the words that are being said. Ralph Waldo Emerson once wrote, "When the eyes say one thing, and the tongue another, a practiced man relies on the language of the first."

7

USING THE LANGUAGE OF SALES TO OVERCOME OBJECTIONS

"If you would persuade, you must appeal to interest rather than intellect."

—Benjamin Franklin

The most challenging buyers to persuade are those who say little or nothing after you present your product. You have no indication of their thoughts or concerns, so you hesitate about which direction to take next. Some won't say anything simply because they have no intention of buying. It happens. However, most will raise an objection or two and give you an idea of which direction you need to go.

Few salespeople mentally jump for joy when they hear objections, but we want you to adopt that habit because people won't object to something if they have no interest in it. Objections equal interest. Repeat that phrase out loud: Objections equal interest.

That's why you should get excited when you hear them. You've invested too much research, energy, and preparation in your presentation to give up.

What are buyers really saying when they voice objections? They may be telling you, "Hey, I'm interested, but I need more information." They may mean, "The product you're presenting is great, but the way you're suggesting I purchase it is not." Or, they may be telling you, "I want it... just not today."

As professional problem-solvers, it's our job to gain a clear understanding of what holds people back from purchasing our products, and to use the language of sales to help buyers rationalize decisions they want to make. You see, most decisions are not made logically. They are made emotionally, then defended or rationalized with logic.

How the Untrained Address Concerns

To give you a blatant example of what happens when you don't understand how to effectively handle buyer concerns with the language of sales, let's consider the following dialog by an untrained salesperson.

Al:	"Hi, folks. (Shakes hands vigorously.) Glad to meet you, and welcome to *Everyone's Carpet*. Is there anything I can show you tonight?"
Bob:	"We're just looking."
Al:	"Well, make yourself at home. How about a nice Berber carpet? We're selling a lot of it these days, so I can get you a good price."
Laurie:	"No, thanks. We're really just looking."

Al: "Oh, okay. (He steps back for a while, but soon he is by their side again.) Yes, that's a beautiful piece of carpet you're looking at there. Bet that would look good in your living room. You know, you folks, sure look familiar to me. Did I sell you carpet before?"

Bob: (By this time, Bob is getting a bit annoyed, but Al fails to read his body language.) "I doubt it."

Laurie: "No, I'm sure you haven't. We've never been in this store before."

Al: "I've worked in several stores in the area. Where did you buy your last carpet?"

Laurie: "We've never bought carpet before."

Al: "Well, here. I'll just follow you around a bit in case you need me. Not everyone is a carpet expert, you know." (Now Al pauses trying to think of what to say next. He feels it's important to fill every moment with conversation.) "So, have you been looking for carpet long?"

Bob: "No, not long."

Al: "Well, we've got the best. I've been selling carpet for over 20 years. I've sold a lot of people in all those years." (Now, Al tries to point out his qualifications.)

Laurie: "We'd really just like to look around on our own. Maybe we could take one of your cards."

Al: (He digs a card out of his jacket pocket.) "Here you go. How much carpet do you need?"

Bob: "We're not sure exactly what we're going to do at this point."

Al: "You folks seem pretty sensible. How about a nice brown, heavy-duty carpet? It's great for young couples. It won't show any stains from all the kid's spills and traffic."

Bob: "The carpet is for my mother."

Al: "Well, do you think she'd like the brown?"

Laurie: "To be honest with you, we are looking on behalf of Bob's mother to give her an idea of who has the best prices. So, we have no intention of buying carpet until she comes with us."

Al: "We are the cheapest in town. Bring your mom in to see me. I can give her a good deal."

As soon as Bob and Laurie are out the door, Al turns to another salesperson and says, "They'll be back. I know I sold them on the fact that we have the cheapest prices in town."

Since you're this far along in the book, we're pretty sure you saw a lot of room for improvement in that dialog, but we'll list the errors anyway to ensure your powers of observation are sharp. What are Al's flaws?

- He came across as a stereotypical salesperson.

- He put himself and his desire to prove himself an expert ahead of the buyer's needs.

- He didn't introduce himself or ask for the buyer's names.

- He asked poor questions. They were irrelevant to the sales process.

- He didn't qualify their N.E.A.D.S.

- He was lost when they expressed their objections.

After you've begun to educate yourself on the strategies of successful selling, you'll more readily recognize poor salesmanship. Once you begin listening to and watching other presentations, you'll be surprised to see how many "Al's" there are in the world of selling. Pay attention and learn from their mistakes.

How the Sales Pro Addresses Concerns

Until you learn how to address buyer concerns, you cannot achieve your full potential in sales. Concerns or objections are a normal part of the sales process. Top pros in sales utilize strategies well. They figure out the patterns and processes related to moving people from one position or line of thought to another and then use that knowledge to help them succeed. When addressing concerns, it is recommended that you:

1. HEAR THEM OUT. Don't interrupt. Don't jump in to answer the concern too quickly. Encourage the buyer to lay it all out. Listen to everything the buyer feels the need to say about your product, presentation, or service. You want to know *everything* they're objecting to. Pay special attention to the words they use when objecting. You'll want to use that same type of language when it's your turn to speak. Listening is your greatest tool. By jumping in too quickly, you could easily create a "me against them" power struggle because no one wants to be proven wrong.

2. ASK FOR FEEDBACK. You may want to rephrase their words slightly rather than mimicking them. "If I understand correctly, your key concerns are...." If you've misunderstood, this is when the buyer will jump in to clarify what they mean. Sometimes they'll answer their own objections, and you won't need the rest of the steps below.

3. QUESTION THE OBJECTION OR CONCERN. Ask the buyer to *elaborate* on their key concerns. You want to determine if those concerns are really all that important or if they're stalling because they feel the decision is too easy or too good to be true. Try to get to the root of what they're *feeling* about the purchasing decision.

4. ANSWER THE OBJECTION. No matter what you sell, your product will have a few weaknesses you'll wish it didn't. Study the weak points of your product and prepare how you'll handle it when those are the objections. In some cases, you will address them simply by acknowledging the weaknesses and comparing them to the greater strengths of the product that will, hopefully, outweigh the bad.

5. CONFIRM THE ANSWER. This is where we separate the average salespeople from the great ones. The pros confirm that their answers to objections have addressed the buyer's concerns. When this step is left undone, it leaves the buyers the opportunity to bring the concern up again, thus stalling the sale further. After answering an objection, simply say, "That clarifies that point, doesn't it?" or "If you agree with that, we can move on." If they don't agree, you may need to go all the way back to step 1 and start over.

6. CHANGE GEARS. Once it's confirmed by the buyers that you've answered their concerns, it's time to mentally, verbally, and in some cases physically, move on. You do this by moving on to the next subject or area of your presentation. You might even say, "By the way…" and then switch topics. This can also be accomplished with a simple click to the next slide or a turn of the page of a proposal. Waving your hand, shifting in your chair, or pointing with a pen are strong uses of body language to signal that you're changing gears. The time may even be right to ask for the business.

Learn and practice these six steps in sequence. The next time you hear an objection, even if it's from your child about not wanting to put their shoes on, break down how you handle it by using these steps and notice the difference in how the situation resolves itself. Then, adapt it to your product or service.

Always be sure to watch your buyers carefully during any objection-handling situation. You don't want to push them into going past an objection if you haven't truly covered it. Their body language will tell you whether they're satisfied with your answer. If you ignore their body language and move on, you'll be doing nothing more than sweeping objections under the carpet. They won't be gone, and they'll very likely re-surface later.

It could happen that your buyers are embarrassed to tell you they don't understand what you said when you thought you handled the objection so smoothly. Instead of going ahead with the sale, they head for the door, and you never learn the real reason why you didn't make the sale.

When you kill an objection, you want to make certain it's dead and not kill the sale along with it.

Strategies for Handling Objections

Here are three ways to help you overcome specific barriers to the sale:

Put the Shoe On the Buyer's Foot

It's common in sales, especially when you are just starting out, to take over an established territory. Let's suppose that is what you are doing. Within a few days, you find out that the salesperson before you didn't leave the position because of the great job they were doing. You are tasked with picking up the pieces and communicating with a lot of unhappy people. When clients are unhappy, they may try to dismiss you because of the negative experience they had with either your product or a previous salesperson.

As an example, let's say you represent National Medical Supplies. Your catalog of products is used by doctor's offices, and your key contacts are typically the office managers. You've just arrived at the office managed by Ron Clark. You no sooner introduce yourself as his new representative than he says, "Thanks for coming by, but we've had such a negative experience with your company that we're looking for another supplier."

Rather than feeling as though you're walking into a lion's den, take charge of the situation. You may, after all, only have a few minutes to save this account. The first thing to do is to apologize. Say, "I'm sorry that has been your experience."

"I'm sorry" are two of the most under-used words—especially in business. Some will say that using them is a sign of weakness. We disagree. Even if you had nothing to do with the client's dissatisfaction, you should be sorry that they had a bad experience with your product or company. It costs you nothing to say it and could very well open the door to reparations.

Dissatisfied or even angry clients can often be calmed just by having someone listen to them. Let them vent. Encourage them to get it all out. At least, they'll still be talking with you, right? "Venting" is a way of releasing steam, and once it's released, the pressure is relieved. The same definition applies when we're talking about verbal venting.

Your next step is to help the buyer put themselves in your shoes or those of the higher-ups at the company. Say, "I understand your unhappiness with the challenges you've had. May I have your permission to just ask you one quick question?" Since you're being so polite, most people will agree to one question.

Here's the question: "If you were the president of National Medical Supplies, and you learned of the situation you've had, what would you do?" Once you ask that question, remain silent. Wait for the answer.

In these situations, buyers will say one of two things:

1. "I'd fire the sales rep."
2. "I'd find a way to offer better products."

After you've "heard him out," reply.

1. "As you can see by my presence here today, that rep is no longer servicing your account. I understand that we'll have to work very hard to regain your trust and confidence and would appreciate the opportunity to continue to serve your needs. You have my commitment, and that of the higher-ups at National Medical Supplies, to give you the first-rate service you deserve."
2. If your company has made a commitment to providing better products, continue with: "And that's exactly why I'm here today." Go on to explain briefly any company initiatives to improve quality. End by requesting the opportunity to at least show him what's new.

Don't go into any lengthy explanations. You are not trying to make a product sale at this point. You're just selling the opportunity to continue to serve (as opposed to being kicked out of the office.)

If the client still shows obvious annoyance with you or your company, suggest ending the meeting but leaving the door open for a future contact. "Ron, I understand your hesitation to move forward. All I'm asking for is to be re-considered as a supplier. I'm happy to compete against others you may be considering and prove to you that we at National Medical Supplies *can* make you happy." If he agrees, get a confirmation for when you will get their list of needs and when they intend to make a decision about suppliers. Then, do your job of providing the level of service he expects and deserves.

Immediately following this type of encounter, send the decision-maker—and anyone else you met—a thank you note for their time and consideration. Let them know you appreciate their honesty about the situation and the opportunity to continue to do business with them. Top sales pros use the language of sales to display their sincere empathy for client situations and desire to serve them well.

Change Their Base

There will be times when a buyer presents an objection you just can't overcome. Rather than attempting to take that objection head-on, it may be preferable to direct the buyer to the positive advantages of your product and help them see how those advantages outweigh the concern. To do this, you would... ask a question. Your question will highlight that major benefit and, hopefully, dwarf objections to the point where they become quite minor in the overall decision process.

This strategy is often used by parents with fussy little ones. You're probably already familiar with it but may not have used it in business situations. For parents, this strategy involves the art of distraction. When a child is fussy because they can't have what they want, parents will offer something else. They present the substitution as something more desirable—and immediate—that resolves the child's immediate need.

Please don't think we're teaching you to treat your buyers like children. We're just suggesting that the objections presented by buyers may not be so strong that they can't be overcome by something else that's very positive. Help the buyer see that what seems so important may not amount to much in the overall scheme of things.

Here's an example from the automotive industry:

You've demonstrated a vehicle to a couple that meets the needs expressed by them. As you begin walking toward the desk where you'll review the financing, the husband raises the objection, "The trunk is too small." The conversation may continue like this:

> You: "I understand that the size of the trunk can be quite important. What is it you intend to put in the trunk that has a size requirement?"
>
> Husband: "Nothing in particular. The trunk just looks small to me."

By feeding the objection back to the buyer, you'll gain a better understanding of his concern. With a vague answer like his, he may just be stalling the sale. You'll want to overcome the concern and find out if there's anything else that's holding him back.

> You: "The trunk in that car is typical for a mid-sized vehicle, which is what you indicated you wanted. If you have a need for a specific size trunk, we may need to eliminate this vehicle from consideration, even though you seemed to like everything else about it. Tell me, what will you base your final decision on—the size of the trunk or the fuel economy, handling,

safety features, or the total amount that you said was so important when we first began looking?"

Do you see how the weight has been put on everything else but the size of the trunk? In essence, you're telling the buyer that they may need to give up some of those other features in order to get a larger trunk. You don't, of course, come right out and say that. You gently suggest it. If the trunk size alters their options to a full-sized vehicle that is more money, that alone may be the tipping point in decision-making. Your goal is to have the benefits they want outweigh any concerns. If the size of the trunk was truly key to the decision, they would have likely mentioned that upfront, and you would have presented a different vehicle.

Here's another example. You're with a buyer who is considering your home exercise equipment.

> **Buyer:** "One of my major concerns is that I'd really like to have a machine that gives me a good workout and doesn't have lots of extras that I don't need."
>
> **You:** "That's good to know. However, you might be interested to know that many of our customers tell us as they achieve a higher level of fitness, and that they get great benefit from additional features. Janie, what will you base your decision on, the four or five extra features, or the opportunity to improve your physical condition in the privacy of your own home?"

Here is where you want to repeat back to the customer what they've told you about their desire for getting in better shape. If the buyer still hesitates over the extra features, you might eliminate the concern by saying, "This model is about the same amount as other brands without some of those added features. Even if *you* don't use them, if you eventually sell the equipment, you'll be able to ask more for it because of the extra features."

Changing the base or showing them a different perspective can often save a sale that otherwise might have been stalled by an objection.

The Guarantee

It's interesting that few salespeople take advantage of the benefit of a money-back guarantee. If your company offers one, learn exactly what it is, and put it in the forefront of your mind. It will save sales that might otherwise be lost when buyers want to shop around. You would take advantage of it this way:

Buyers enter your store and settle near one of your home entertainment centers. You introduce yourself and offer to answer their questions about it. During your discussion, you qualify them as to their needs, size specifications, and the amount they expect to invest. You also learn two important things: 1) They are a couple, and 2) They want that entertainment center. Yet, at the end of your presentation, when you ask how soon you can have it delivered, they say, "Thanks for your time. We'll think about it and let you know."

What does "I'll let you know," really mean in cases like this? It usually means, "Now that I've found what I want, I'm going to shop around and see if I can find it any cheaper." So, their concern is "the money," and you want to save this sale.

Here's what to say:

You:	"That's smart of you, Kelly. You wouldn't mind if I ask a couple more questions before you go, would you? They might save you some time and money."

"Time" and "money" will almost always get the attention of your buyers. No one wants to waste either of them, right?

You:	"Are you impressed with the overall quality of this particular entertainment center?"
Buyer:	"Oh, yes."
You:	"Then it's the right size for the space you have in mind?"
Buyer:	"It's just the right size."
You:	"And, you mentioned that you like the simplicity of the entire system—nothing too elaborate, correct?"

Gently list all the things they were pleased with. Remind them that you service everything you sell. You have free delivery and installation. Oh, and don't forget to mention the liberal credit terms available to them—whatever your company offers.

In some cases, you'll be able to help them own the equipment by striking a responsive chord with some of the services that you can offer. If not, you'll be able to get down to the final objection, which is usually money. When you get them to agree that the reason they won't buy is money, you've isolated their real concern.

Most people will want to shop for a better price. In some businesses, it's common practice to agree to match any other price on the identical product they can find within 30 days. This often gets the buyer to commit to making the purchase with the intention of looking around further but being able to enjoy its use now.

This is a very low-risk proposition since once the buyer owns your product, they tend to move their focus toward other more pressing needs and stop shopping.

You might say something like this, "We could have you enjoying this beautiful home entertainment system within 24 hours and still assure you that as you shop around, we'll match any lower price you might find on this identical unit. Our clients love this guarantee, and I must admit, every now and then, even as economical as we are, we do have to honor that guarantee. We're happy to do it, though, because we know you want the lowest price, with the least amount of hassle. Should I set up a morning or afternoon delivery for you, so you can start enjoying this entertainment center while still having the opportunity to shop around?"

You're encouraging them to do what they said they wanted to do while giving them the benefits of enjoying your product. This is what it means to create win-win situations in sales.

Now that we've covered how to get past the most common stalls, let's move on to getting commitments and closing sales.

8

THE LANGUAGE OF CLOSING

It does happen that people go ahead quickly with making commitments or agreeing to purchases once their concerns have been addressed. However, more often than not, people need an extra nudge to make that commitment. This is the "closing" step of the sales process. You'll continue to use the language of sales where you build pictures of ownership and speak as if they already own your product. However, since this step is the grand finale in the sales process, there will be times when it requires some special touches.

A survey was conducted years ago with follow up calls made to interested buyers who didn't end up buying. You might be surprised to learn that when asked for reasons why they didn't buy, most said, "We were never asked." In other words, they weren't clearly and directly asked for the sale. Wow! What a shame! The salespeople they worked with did 98 percent of their jobs—persuading the buyers of the value of their product—and stopped there. As mentioned before, those salespeople made it easy for the next salesperson to close the sale.

We don't want that to happen to you. So, the purpose of this chapter is to teach you the key points of closing sales and a few strategies that have been proven successful in all types of sales.

Do's and Don'ts

When it's time to move into the closing step of the sales process, do so smoothly. This is not a time to change your demeanor or speed up the pace. Any drastic change could cause the buyers to hesitate or to go back to building that wall of sales resistance that you've broken down.

Even the act of pulling out paperwork or pulling up an agreement on your screen could interrupt the flow of the sales process. It's best if you've had it already within reach (or on your screen in the background) to make the transition much smoother. Ideally, you would have already been adding notes to an agreement throughout the process. If your buyers see this and try to stop you, you would simply say, "I understand your concern, Julie. What I'd like to do is outline our thoughts as we discuss your situation. Then, if it makes sense, we'll go ahead, okay?" Or, you might say, "I find that when I take good notes, I don't miss anything that's important to you or that could save you money should you go ahead. I do that on the paperwork so it's all in one place for us to review later."

Once your paperwork is complete, scan it, showing concern for accuracy. Then, smile as you turn it toward your buyers for their review and approval. At this point, you might say, "Sam, analyzing all considerations, I sincerely feel this decision makes good sense. And, with your approval right here (point), I'll begin giving you the finest service possible."

Then, the most important "do" in closing: When you've asked your final closing question, stop talking. The onus is on the buyers to either go ahead with the purchase, or to bring up anything else that's on their minds about the purchase. If you break the silence by speaking first, you've stalled the moment of decision. And you never want to do that!

Everyone Loves a Good Story

Good stories engage us both mentally and emotionally, don't they? That's the type of engagement we want from our buyers. We want them so involved in this last step of the sales process that they can't imagine themselves not enjoying the benefits of our products.

These "stories" are called "sales closes." We will provide you some here, but you will develop others from your own experiences in sales. You'll hear some memorable ones from other sales pros and incorporate them into your arsenal of strategies as well.

You'll tell stories of other people with similar challenges who purchased your products and are very happy they did. You may have stories about those who didn't purchase when you first met with them and were so unhappy with another supplier that they came back to you for help. The idea behind the stories is to help people who can benefit most from your product to make that final decision to go ahead. Sales stories help people overcome fear or procrastination or both when making ownership decisions.

Your own stories may do the job of getting people past the tipping point to where they "authorize" your "paperwork," but until you build a library of stories, here are some that you can use.

1. The Similar Situation Close

The first type of close is called the Similar Situation Close. This is where you simply share the story of other people with similar needs who went ahead with owning your product and are very happy that they did. It might sound like this:

Sales Pro: "John, Jennifer, I understand you're hesitant about the financial commitment of buying a home when you have your first baby on the way. I was helping another couple about a year ago who felt the same way. They just couldn't decide.

One day, we looked at a great home and they fell in love with it. When I asked them if they were ready to begin the process of owning it, the husband was ready, but the wife started thinking it might be too big for them. She thought maybe they should rethink it and go for a small starter home.

Well, they ended up going ahead on the larger home and were so happy they did. They had no idea how much space the baby's things would take up. And, now they're thinking ahead to having another child and are happy they won't have to move again to fit that child into their home.

Now, you'd like to be settled before this baby comes, wouldn't you?"

John: "Yes. We certainly don't want to move close to when the baby arrives or even shortly after. We'll have enough other things going on then."

Sales Pro:	"In order to get you settled by the date you have in mind, it's important to make a decision soon. What you told me you liked about this home is that it's a single story; that it's on a quiet street; and that it's not too far from your family. The kitchen appliances are all relatively new, which they weren't in some of the other homes we looked at. Basically, this home is move-in ready based on the needs you have. Are you ready to go ahead with an offer?"

With this similar situation story, you've helped your clients overcome their fears to rationalize a decision they really wanted to make.

Note the use of a "yes or no" question at the end of that close. You're no longer using open questions to gather information. It's time to get specific, direct answers to close the sale.

2. The Competitive Edge Close

In a business-to-business situation, you may lean a bit more on facts and logic than on emotion. There is emotion in play, though, as no one wants to make a poor business decision or let the competition get ahead of them. Here's what to say to implement the Competitive Edge Close. "Mr. Ruiz, please realize that many of your competitors are facing the same challenges today that you are. I see it all the time in relation to the products I represent. Isn't it interesting when an entire industry is fighting the same forces, some companies do a better job of meeting those challenges than others? (Pause for his answer.) My entire objective here today has been to provide you with a competitive edge.

Gaining a competitive edge, no matter how large or small, just makes good business sense, doesn't it?"

Who's going to say "no" to gaining an edge over the competition? No one. You've already done the job of demonstrating how your product will enhance his business. All you need now is the purchase order number, deposit, or an endorsement of your agreement. When the Mr. Ruiz's of the world agree that gaining that edge makes good business sense, it's time to ask for his final approval to go ahead with the purchase.

3. The Secondary Question Close

With this strategy, you're going to pose the major decision with your closing question. Then, without pausing, you ask another question that's an alternate of choice question that can only be answered if the buyer is seeing themselves owning your product. This is a little more complex to explain, so here's an example of it in use:

"Can we agree, Dan, the only decision we have to make today is how soon you'll start enjoying these wonderful golf clubs? By the way, will you be playing public courses, or do you belong to a private club?"

With either answer, public or private, Dan is seeing himself on the golf course... with his new clubs.

Here's another example with a service instead of a physical product:

As I see it, Darlene, the only decision we have to make today is how soon you'll start enjoying the increased productivity of your employees when they start using this equipment. By the way, will you want us to train them all at once, or train just a few and let them train the others?"

When the training question is answered, the purchase of the equipment is carried.

This strategy can be easily adapted to any product or service. It just takes a little thought and practice to get it under your belt. Let's step through it now.

The major decision is introduced with these words: "As I see it, the only decision we have to make today is how soon..." or "Can we agree, the only decision we have to make today is how soon ..."

The major decision is then followed, without pause, by the Secondary Question that you introduce by saying, "By the way..."

To use the Secondary Question successfully, you must:

1) State the major decision in terms of a benefit to the client.

"The only decision...is how soon you'll start enjoying (the benefit)." Never pose the major decision in negative terms: "...how soon you'll stop throwing away money by..." Or, even worse, a thinly disguised attempt at humor: "...how soon you'll get on the ball and start saving money by ordering from me."

2) Avoid any pause between posing the major decision and asking the Secondary Question.
3) State the Secondary Question in terms of an alternate of choice question.
4) Deliver the words in a relaxed and alert manner.

Practice this strategy until you can use it clearly and casually. The casual approach is the cornerstone of sales success. By casual, I do not mean careless. You must cultivate an alert but relaxed attitude that makes people feel comfortable.

4. The Purchase Order Close

This can also be called "The Paperwork Close." It's one of the simplest closes to use in either business-to-business sales or business-to-consumer situations. In a business situation, you would simply say, "What purchase order number will be assigned to this requisition?" When the buyer gives you a number, all that's left is to ask for their signature. If they say they don't know, ask, "What's the process to find out?"

With consumers, you would say, "With your approval right here on the paperwork, Anna, we'll get your order processed and delivery scheduled."

5. The Sharp Angle Close

This close carries the porcupine questioning technique to a higher level of effectiveness. Instead of merely answering a question with a question as with the standard porcupine, answer with one that, if they reply the way their original question indicates they will, they're going ahead with the purchase.

> Buyer: "If I decide I want this boat, can you handle delivery in time for Memorial weekend?"
>
> You: "Are you telling me that if I *can* deliver this boat in time for Memorial weekend that you're ready to make the purchase today?"

To use the Sharp-Angle method, you must first have your buyer make a demand or express a specific desire that you know you can meet. You would only use this as a closing strategy. If used earlier in the sales process, it could be considered pushy or aggressive.

6. Weighing The Facts

When your buyers are hesitant and stall by saying, "We just want to weigh the facts," they may think they're sending you packing. But, as a pro who has mastered the language of sales, you'll be ready to help them to the next step in the process with this close.

We'll use real estate for the example, but the strategy can be applied to any product. Your goal is to help them do the "weighing" to reach the point of making an obvious decision. Note: You would only use this strategy when you know your solution is truly good for the buyer and that you've eliminated other options through your conversations with them.

Kevin and Kaycee Smith have looked at several homes and seem to have settled on one as being best suited for their needs. They're just afraid to take the leap into ownership. Their fear is causing them to stall making the decision they know they want to make. It's your job to help them rationalize the decision.

> You: "Of all the homes we've seen, it seems you're most excited about the home on Third Street. Is that right?"
>
> Kevin: "We really do like it, but it's a pretty big investment. I don't know that we're ready to make a decision on it right now."
>
> You: "I understand. It *is* a big decision, and it's important to feel good about making it. Could it possibly be that you're feeling you haven't had a chance to weigh the facts?"
>
> Note that when you suggest this, most people will jump on it to relieve the pressure they're feeling about going ahead. This is natural and to be expected in many sales situations.

Kevin:	"Yes. I think that's it. We really want to analyze the details before deciding."
You:	"I understand how you feel, and weighing the facts before making a decision makes a lot of sense. In fact, when I'm in this type of situation, I use a simple method. You wouldn't mind if I show you, would you?"
Kaycee:	"I guess not."
You:	"Great! Thank you. First, I draw a simple scale. Please don't laugh at my artistic abilities."

Here are a couple of versions you can use:

 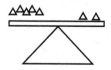

You:	"On the left side of the scale, I pile up, just like small weights, the reasons I feel it makes good sense to go ahead. On the right side of the scale, I pile up reasons I feel are against it. Then, I simply add up the reasons on each side to see which decision is best."

The important thing here is to keep going with the flow of the conversation, rather than try to rigidly stick with a set of words you've memorized.

You:	"Why don't we try it together, so you don't miss any important details. We've considered a lot of properties, haven't we?"

Kaycee:	"I guess it wouldn't hurt. We *have* looked at a lot of homes."
You:	"Wonderful. This won't take long. Let's start with reasons favoring the decision for the home on Third. You liked the open floor plan, right?"
Kaycee:	"Yes, it feels so much bigger than our current home."
Kevin:	"And it has the four bedrooms we want. And the three-car garage."
You:	"You liked that the kids could walk to the neighborhood school. No bussing or having to drive them, right?"
Kaycee:	"Yes, that's important."
Kevin:	"It's not too far from work for either of us."
You:	"Right! Kevin, you also liked the low mainte-nance landscaping."
Kevin:	"Absolutely. I'd rather enjoy my yard than spend hours working in it."
You:	"It's well within your price range."
Kaycee:	"I really like the kitchen. There's room for us to cook together. Our current kitchen is too small for that."
You:	"Cooking as a family is fun, isn't it? We're up to eight weights in favor of the home. What else comes to mind?"
Kaycee:	"We wouldn't have to do much to it before moving in—maybe some painting in the kids' rooms. They all have favorite colors."
You:	"Okay. What would you say are your con-cerns—things that would keep you from mov-ing into this home?"
Kevin:	"Well, we had hoped for a home with a pool."

You:	"Okay. What else?"
Kaycee:	"We'd have to sell our home before we could come up with the down payment."
You:	"If you have no other concerns, we're looking at eight yeses and only two nos. It looks like the answer is rather obvious, doesn't it?"

Expect to wait in silence now. One of three things will happen: 1) They'll stall by asking for more time or changing the subject. 2) They'll decide to go ahead. 3) They'll come up with another objection to drag out the process.

Kevin:	"Well, we're the kind of people who really need to think it over."

Please note that most of the time, you will need to use several closing strategies before you get a final agreement. This is to be expected. That is why we're offering so many closes in this book. Your goal is to know more ways to ask for the sale than the buyer knows how to say "no." Let's help Kevin and Kaycee "think it over."

7. The "I Want to Think it Over" Close

You:	"That's fine, Kevin. Obviously, you wouldn't take the time to think it over unless you were seriously interested, would you?"
Kaycee:	"We're seriously interested. We need a larger home. It's just hard to know we're making the right decision.
You:	"I understand. Since you are interested, may I assume you'll give it very careful consideration?"
Kevin:	"Of course, we will."
You:	"Just to clarify my thinking, what is it about the house that you want to think over?

Ask about every benefit of the home. Every time they say no, they are that much closer to a yes, aren't they? Kevin and Kaycee answer no to every benefit, so what is it that they want to think over? In most cases, it will come down to money. Either the home will be too expensive, they won't be comfortable with the large initial investment, or they may be worried about getting qualified for the loan. You need to get them to admit what their real final objection is.

You: "Could it be the financing or even the initial investment that's holding you back?"

Kaycee: "Yes. We might have another baby, and I'm not sure if we should make a financial commitment like this right now."

Now that they've admitted the money is the real concern, you can handle it. It's when the buyer isn't clear on what's holding them back that you will struggle.

8. The Reduction to the Ridiculous Close

Now that you know the final concern is the money, it's time to rationalize it. For most, the "big number" related to a purchase can be overwhelming. It's the monthly amount that most people use to make decisions: "Does it fit into the monthly budget?" So, to help people overcome their fears of that big number, your job is to get them to do the math until you reach a number that makes sense.

When you hear a money objection such as, "It costs too much," or "The price is too high," it's time to ask a question to find out how that amount is causing their hesitation. It can be as simple as asking, "How much 'too much' do you feel it is?"

You see, people aren't expecting to get your product for free. There is an amount they will have in mind that's acceptable. When your product is over that amount, you work with the difference between the two—not the whole amount. Once your client admits the difference that's giving them pause, get out the calculator and have them do the following math:

1. Determine about how long the buyer will benefit from your offering. It could be three months or 30 years, depending on the product. Divide the amount by that number of years to get an annual amount for the difference.
2. Divide the annual amount by 12 for a monthly amount.
3. Divide the annual amount by 52 weeks to get the weekly amount.
4. Divide the weekly amount by 5 or 7 days, depending on the buyer's situation. If this is a sale to a business that's open 5 days a week, use the 5. If the sale is to a consumer who might benefit from the product every day, use 7. Now, you have a daily amount.

Usually, the daily amount is sufficiently small for the buyer to rationalize the benefits as being greater. If you're selling products in the manufacturing world, you may have to reduce the amount to an hourly number.

As an example, a major purchase that's $10,000 greater than expected and would be used for 5 years reduces down to $2,000 a year; $167 per month; $38.46 per week; and $7.69 per day (in a 5-day week). When your buyer puts the purchase into perspective as only being $7.69 per day more than they had hoped "for all the benefits discussed," the decision becomes a lot easier.

Champions always do their selling math with a calculator. No matter how confident you are in your mathematical abilities, always use a calculator. Know your formulas and figures so you can quickly provide any numerical information that your buyer might be requesting. A buyer, seeing you punching numbers into your calculator, probably won't question the figures. But, if you start furiously scratching numbers on paper with a pencil, the buyer may grow uncomfortable. Even worse, if you just rattle figures off, they may doubt you. When using this strategy, encourage your buyers to do the math along with you.

1. The Best Things in Life Close

This approach is used when the buyers procrastinate, making the decision to get involved with your product or service.

Salesperson: Isn't it true that the only time you have ever benefitted from anything in your life has been when you have said "yes" instead of "no?" You said "yes" to your marriage (Optional: and I can see how happy you are.) You said "yes" to your job, your home, your car—all the things that I'm sure you truly enjoy. You see, when you say "yes" to me, it's not really me you are saying "yes" to, but all the benefits that we offer, and those are the things you really want for your family, don't you agree?"

2. The "I Can Get it Cheaper" Close

When you hear this stall/concern/objection, be happy. The buyer isn't saying, "I don't want this," are they? They're saying they do! Some will tell you this just to see if you'll lower your price. Others will truly attempt to shop around. To keep them from attempting to buy from someone else, use these words:

"That may well be true, John. And, after all, in today's economy, we all want the most for our money, don't we? (Wait for his answer.)

"A truth that I have learned over the years is that the cheapest price is not always what we really want. Most people look for three things when making an investment:

1. the highest quality
2. the best service, and
3. the lowest amount

I have never yet found a company that could offer the finest quality and the best service for the lowest price. I'm curious, John, for your long-term happiness with this product, which of the three would you be most willing to give up? The finest quality? Excellent service? Or, low price?"

Few people will want to give up quality or service. Most will end up agreeing that they expect to "get what they pay for."

1. The "No" Stall Close

Some people will just say "no" to you without further explanation. Oh, they'll do it kindly, "Well, Bob, we appreciate you for sharing all of this information with us, but we're just not ready to make a decision." This is a stall, but since it's not a "yes," it's also a "no." If you're unable to ferret out anything that will help you move the sale forward, try the phraseology of this close. It goes like this:

> "John and Mary, I appreciate what you're saying. In fact, it could be a nice way of saying 'no.' If so, I'd like to consider those two letters, N and O. The way I see it, 'no' is the first two letters of the word 'nothing.' Meaning, if you say 'no' today, nothing will happen, and things will stay pretty much the same. You'll still have... (do a negative benefit summary

of all the reasons they agreed to talk with you in the first place... all the things they're lacking).

However, if you say 'yes' to what we're suggesting, all those things will change for the better. (Be prepared to do a brief recap of the benefits you have covered.) So, based on that truth, which word seems best for you? 'Yes?' Or, 'No?'"

This close has helped many a buyer realize what they're giving up by stalling and be reminded that they'll still have the "pain" that caused them to speak with the salesperson in the first place. There will be times when a little synopsis is enough to get them off the fence and to agree to get the decision made.

2. The "It's Not in The Budget" Close

You will hear this as a reason not to go ahead in both business and consumer situations. Budgets are inanimate. They are created by decision-makers, right? So, someone controls them. They don't control others. They're simply tools for directing where the money goes. Rather than letting a vague reference to a budget stall the sale, help your buyers rationalize their decision by pointing out who is in control. It might sound like this:

"I can understand that, Jim. That's why I contacted you in the first place. I'm fully aware of the fact that every well-managed business controls the flow of its money with a carefully planned budget. The budget is a necessary tool for every company to give direction to their goals. However, the tool itself doesn't dictate how the company is run. It must be flexible. You, as the controller of that budget, retain for yourself the right to flex that budget in the best interest of the company's financial present and competitive future, don't you?

What we have been examining here today is a system, which will allow your company an immediate and continuing competitive edge. Tell me, under these conditions, will your budget flex, or will it dictate your actions?"

You can switch the words "business" and "company" for family in the case of a consumer sale.

These closes are not meant to talk anybody into anything they don't want or need. Their sole purpose is to help people make decisions they want to make. Remember, they wouldn't invest their valuable time talking with you about your product or service if they didn't have a need. Buyers are just like us. The truth is, very few people are ever talked into or sold something they don't really want. When you put service to your buyer ahead of money, you'll always come out on top.

We have done a lot of selling, and always took buyers' interests to heart. By representing quality products, it becomes our obligation to share it with those who need it most and qualify to own it. If we don't help them, someone else will, and we will have no control over the level of service they receive. When what you're offering is right, do everything you can to help them get over the hills of fear and procrastination.

Let's turn the tables on this conversation for a moment. Drawing on your own experience as a buyer, have you appreciated sales professionals who helped you make a decision? Have you been happy enough to recommend those sales professionals to others? Of course, you have! We all have. Set a goal to become someone people would not hesitate to recommend. Become someone buyers seek out as an expert in your field.

The End is Really a Beginning

Creating the opportunity to close sales starts at the beginning of the transaction—when you first contact buyers. If you are weak on original contact, qualifying, handling objections, presentations, or any other area of the sales process or are generally weak in asking pertinent questions, you are costing your buyer, yourself, and your company a lot of money, loss of time and aggravation. The simple fact is no one closes every sale, but just think of how much better you can become when you put your best effort into it. A perfect ending needs a perfect beginning.

By mastering and then implementing the skills in this book, you will prove yourself to be a truly professional salesperson. The true pros are the cream of the crop and earn the highest incomes because they deserve them. They've earned them with the high level of service they provide.

Close With Empathy

Now that you've learned a few closes to use, let's talk about the spirit in which they're to be delivered. They should be delivered with empathy. Empathy is defined as: Understanding intimately the feelings, thoughts, and motives of another because you have experienced it yourself or can put yourself "in their shoes." This is different, yet often confused with sympathy. When you're sympathetic, you understand the other person's feelings.

With empathy, you can mentally put yourself in the shoes of another to understand how to proceed in each situation. Situations will vary depending on the information each buyer shares with you. Until you develop empathy for buyers, you may struggle more than is necessary in sales. When you can demonstrate a sincere concern for their needs and a commitment to providing a satisfactory solution, selling will get easier and more rewarding.

As a professional salesperson, you must truly believe that you can satisfy the buyer's needs. You must see the benefits, features, and limitations of your product or service from you're their point of view; you must weigh things on their scale of values, not your own; you must realize what is important to the buyer.

When to Close

There's a certain electricity in the air when buyers are ready to go ahead, but it may take you a while to learn how to tune in to it. While you're developing your skills, here are some other things to watch for:

- The buyers have been moving along at a certain pace, and suddenly, they slow the pace way down. They're likely slowing down to think it over because they're feeling motivated to go ahead.

- The buyers speed up the pace. Now that they've made the decision, they're excited and want to get on with it.

- The buyers ask technical questions. These are questions they'll only need the answer to when they own the product.

When you recognize these signs, ask what's called a "test closing question." It's a way of getting a confirmation that the buyers are ready to move forward. Without that confirmation, you could move into the closing step prematurely and kill the sale. A test closing question can be as simple as, "Kate, how are you feeling about this so far?" When you get a positive response, you'll know it's time to close. If there's any hesitation, ask more questions to clarify what might be holding the buyer back. As you get more experience in selling, you will become more proficient at reading buying signs.

Unfortunately, there isn't one closing strategy that will work every time. Even if there was one that worked 25% of the time, so many people would jump on it, the overuse would kill it within a very short time. So, it's essential that you learn multiple ways to ask for the sale.

Get Comfortable With No

You must learn to understand and be comfortable with hearing the word "no" to reach the Champion level in selling. A Champion knows that the "say no first" reflex of all buyers is their source of security. The "no" that buyers flip out so easily is the raw material you will polish and refine into your success.

Know that you'll hear the word "no" every day of your career and learn to recognize the enormous potential behind every no. Throw yourself into learning how to convert those negatives into positives. That's what this book and your success is all about: Turning "no" into "yes" using the language of sales. The highest-paid professionals never stop practicing, improving, and adding to their selling skills. Nothing will do more to improve your sales performance than having a collection of effective sales tools that you've practiced until you can deliver them without thinking.

9

SELLING YOURSELF

"The most important sale you'll ever make
is to the person you see in the mirror every
day—yourself!"

—Tom Hopkins

If you woke up every single day with the goal of giving your best in
every area of your life, what would that look like for you? Do you
typically operate in a *reactive* manner—reacting to whatever pops
up via phone, email, text, or random thought? Or do you develop
a solid plan for each day—allowing for those inevitable challenges
or opportunities that pop up? Stop reading for a moment and
give this some serious thought. Don't generalize. Think about
the specifics of how this very day is going.

When you get in the habit of developing a solid plan for each
day, you will be able to get on a track that will lead to the achievement of your goals, both personal and in your sales career. With
a daily plan, you'll constantly remind yourself of those goals and

the individual steps required to achieve them. Not only will you remind yourself of your goals, but you'll also be providing yourself with daily confidence that you can have whatever you set your mind to once you break it down into manageable steps. Isn't that fabulous?

We have witnessed many sales careers devastated because the salespeople were unable to believe in their own potential for success. They sabotaged themselves by living with low, poor, or negative self-esteem.

What is Self-Esteem?

Simplified, it's what you think of yourself. It's your opinion of you. It includes how you see yourself as a child, a sibling, a spouse, friend, student, sales professional, athlete, driver, businessperson, investor, hobbyist, etc.

The important thing to realize is that your opinion of yourself in each of those areas dictates how you act in every situation you encounter. And even more importantly, your opinion can and may change with every experience you have. The best news of all is that you have the ability to alter your perspective and the way you feel about yourself. In fact, you are the only one who can choose how you think about yourself.

You may be wondering about some of the areas in your life that may not be so positive. Surely, you wouldn't choose to let a negative perspective develop, would you? The programming begins at birth, and then we have little control over how we react to it. However, later in life, negative self-esteem may develop by default—by simply failing to exercise control over what goes into your mind.

What about those notorious sayings we've all heard (or maybe even said) such as, "It's my nature." "I've always been that way." If you've come to believe this about yourself, you can also come to STOP believing this about yourself—and the sooner you begin, the faster you'll become a champion in every area of your life.

Low self-esteem can be a real drain not only on your career, but on every aspect of your life. You will defeat yourself before you ever contact potential clients. And, no surprise here, they'll sense your defeated attitude before you even speak. Your entire manner is affected by your self-esteem.

Hopefully, this knowledge plants a seed of awakening in you; a realization that you can break the chains of limitations you've put on yourself so far in life. Let's get started!

Invest a few moments with a pad of paper or a fresh document on your computer and list all the aspects of your life that are truly important to you. These might include being a good spouse, an involved parent, a good tennis player, or whatever. Then, rate yourself in each area on a 1 to 10 scale with 10 being "terrific." Don't take too much time to think about it. Just write down the number that comes to mind.

Once you've completed the list, go back to each item, and write down the rating you'd like to have for each. Then, close your eyes. Envision yourself at that higher rating. What does it feel like? If you're like most people, it will feel wonderful! Hold onto that feeling and believe that you have the ability to achieve those higher ratings. You *can* change. You *can* become that person... with a high self-esteem.

You see, we become (or get) what we think about most. If we see ourselves as average income-earners, guess what happens when we have an exceptional month in sales? The following month will likely be below average. Thus, we'll maintain our "average" income over a period of time. When we envision and create the feelings of someone who earns an above-average income, our results will change. We will act like those above-average salespeople. We will do what's required to learn the skills of the "above-average." We'll read the books, practice the skills, and utilize our new learning to the best of our abilities. We will reach out to the bigger clients those folks are comfortable with. We will start living in that world—and being comfortable there.

If there was a child in your life who had low self-esteem, you'd build them up, wouldn't you? You'd work with them. You'd pay attention to their attitudes daily. You'd help them learn skills to become happy and fulfilled. So, why not do it for yourself?

What are you Telling Yourself?

We all have little voices inside our heads. Those voices are the ones that virtually slap us on our foreheads when we do or say something dumb or dumber. They're the voices that replay (sometimes a million times over) what someone said to or about us. They're also the voices that either encourage or discourage us to reach out and connect with someone, whether it's in a business or personal situation. They're the voices that constantly judge, whine, and complain.

Have you ever caught yourself thinking or saying, "If only…?"

"If only I could get a better break."
"If only I had more money/time/friends."
"If only, I'd chosen a different life partner."
"If only I worked for a better company."
"If only I was smarter."

Those statements demonstrate a lack of personal accountability created by an acceptance of the negative reinforcement offered up by those little voices. When we allow ourselves to live with "if only" excuses, we hold ourselves back. If you've never heard this before, hear it now: No one else can hold us back *unless we give them permission to do so.* It's critical to your success to pay attention to what you're telling yourself.

Those voices also provide some positive input. They tell us, "I'm really good at _____." Fill in the blank for yourself with things like sports, math, writing, connecting with others, whatever it is you know you're good at. Sadly, for most of us, those little voices default to the negative more than the positive.

Most people go through life just accepting what those voices say. They don't give the negative input much thought. They just accept it, shrug it off as "that's the way it is," and live their lives wishing and dreaming for more. High achievers understand that they control those voices. They actively create positive messages that lead to higher self-esteem and self-motivation. They train the voices to become their positive coaches, providing encouragement—in essence, selling themselves on being, doing, having, and getting more out of life.

Rather than mentally slapping your forehead for something you could have said or said differently, consider every situation to be a lesson. Be *proactive* instead of *reactive*. Tell yourself, "Next time I'm in a situation like that, I will…" and then fill in the rest of that sentence with a positive statement. Repeat it to yourself several times to get those little voices to add that to their repertoire of internal messages. You don't have to live with regret when you can turn nearly any situation into a learning opportunity for a better future.

The American televangelist Joel Osteen once said, "It's easy to get negative because you get beat down. You go through a few disappointments, and it's easy to stay in that negative frame of mind. Choosing to be positive and having a grateful attitude is a whole cliché, but your attitude is going to determine how you're going to live your life." So, it's not what others believe about your success that matters, it's what you believe. Your belief begins with the internal conversations and expectations you set for your external results. Let's start by looking at some of the internal conversations people have with themselves every day.

Imagine if you are overweight or out of shape physically, and you wake up every morning saying something to yourself like, "I don't even want to look at myself in the mirror." Or maybe it's, "You will never meet the woman (or man) of your dreams looking like this." These are negative statements, aren't they? Of course, you could throw much more colorful words in there to make these thoughts even more negative, but you get the point. Is this type of internal conversation likely to lead to anything positive in your mind or in your life? Of course, it won't.

The fact is that we see many people every day who struggle with their weight for a variety of reasons, some of which they may have little control over, such as having a health challenge, and they choose to beat themselves up like this on a daily basis. You may even be one of them.

Let's look at a different approach that allows you to have a positive internal conversation that leads to better external results. Zig Ziglar referred to this in one of his talks. He said, "I was intentionally overweight for many years of my life. The reason I say *intentionally* is because I was never force-fed a single meal in my life."

When you read that, what comes to your mind? What should come to your mind is that like Zig suggested here, he had total control over the situation the whole time regarding the food choices that were made. In your case or in the case of others, it may not just be food choices, right? It could be food choices, exercise choices, and even lifestyle choices that lead to people being overweight and out of shape.

Are you Ready for the Good News?

If you had the power to create the result you have now, in this case, being overweight, you have the same power, with different habits, to create a different result. So instead of telling yourself internally something negative about your current situation, tell yourself something positive knowing that you have the power to create any result you want when you change your approach. Tell yourself, "Each and every day, I have the power to improve the way I look and the way I feel by taking control of my choices." You can also use, "I have the ability, more than anyone else in the world, to empower myself to do everything of which I am capable."

With both of these internal statements, notice that they are phrased in the positive. Focus on your ability to take and keep control in everything you do, and most importantly, don't require approval from anyone else to get started. This gives you all the power you need to begin immediately to go to work on making any changes you want in any area of your life.

The actor Jim Carrey once noted that, "So many of us choose our path out of fear disguised as practicality. What we really want seems impossibly out of reach and ridiculous to expect, so we never ask the universe for it." Do you feel that way about what you want in your life?

Go back to what we just talked about and create an internal conversation that you can have with yourself every single day, even multiple times each day, so you never again feel like anything that could be possible for someone else is not possible for you. Remember, with billions of people on this earth, nobody else will ever be you. You are a unique individual. With that said, what are you going to do, starting right now that will lead you to become the absolute best you can be in every area of your life?

Ten Steps To Creating Positive Internal Conversations

1. Make Every Internal Statement Positive Instead of Negative.

No matter where you are in your life right now, creating negative internal conversations will do you no good. The only way you are going to create a positive reality is to change your internal conversations. You may be going through an extremely difficult time right now, and it may not just be in one area, but multiple areas of your life. Does that mean you can't change everything you see as negative? Of course, it doesn't. All it means is that you have to adjust your thinking in order to find solutions. Albert Einstein once said, "You can never solve a problem with the same thinking that created it." This means you need to use a new perspective to focus on solutions and not on the challenge or challenges you are facing.

2. Always Look at Past Failures As Opportunities to Grow and Learn From Mistakes Instead of As Negative Events that Hold You Back.

We have all made mistakes that have led to failures in the past. We will make mistakes in the future that can lead to failures in one or more areas of our lives, too. The key is to continue to remind yourself that the past doesn't have any control over what you choose to do right now. Only you have control over that. Embrace that control, and start writing down words and phrases that will build you up and not break you down. The past is behind you, and you can only live in the now, so don't let another second go by allowing anything to hold you back from being your absolute best.

3. Choose and Use Positive Action Words in Your Internal Conversations to Stimulate Movement in the Direction You Want to Go.

What are some action words that will stimulate you to start moving in a direction that you know will change your life in the most incredible ways possible? Use words like dynamic, significant, meaningful, awakening, propelling, and persuasive to get yourself started. Here are some examples for you:

"I am dynamic in everything I do, and I will continue to stimulate the world around me."

"I am significant not only in what I am doing now, but in everything I will do in the future."

"My life is meaningful not just because of what it will do for me, but also because of my ability to positively impact others."

"Each day, I experience an awakening of my body, my soul, and my spirit that allows me to create incredible results in everything I do."

"By staying positive and focusing on being my best today, I am creating the best chance of propelling myself into the future that I want."

"Each and every day, I become more and more persuasive with myself and all of those I meet as I evolve in every single way possible."

Can you see how simply choosing and using positive words like these in your internal conversations makes you feel unstoppable and capable of doing anything you set your mind to?

4. Focus Your Internal Conversations on One Area at a Time So You Can Complete The Tasks You Set for Yourself Without Being Overwhelmed.

Remember that these conversations begin internally, but quickly allow the commands that you are now giving your subconscious mind to move into the conscious mind. These thoughts move you to take action and produce results externally. This requires a simple formula that includes: preparation, process, and production. You prepare your subconscious first and then your conscious mind. Follow the process of completing the tasks you have set for yourself. That will lead to you producing the results you set out to produce.

5. Give Yourself Room to Make Adjustments, but Not Excuses.

The best thing you can do for yourself as you continually go through these steps is to allow for ebbs and flows and the unexpected with the idea that you will *respond* to adversity versus *reacting* to it. However, you never want to allow yourself, regardless of what happens, to make excuses when things become challenging. A true champion makes adjustments, never excuses.

6. Never Settle for Being Just "Good Enough."

Make your goals big enough that you will never stop working toward improving every area of your life. You have so much ability that you may not even be aware of. Once you start feeling like you are good enough at something, whether in your personal or professional life, you will likely stop working as hard, stop learning as much, and stop giving your best. Always work on improving in every area of your life.

7. Focus on Small Achievements Today that Will Lead to Big Accomplishments Tomorrow.

Each big goal in your life should be broken down into smaller actionable steps so you can see the progress you're making toward achieving them. For example, if your goal is to earn $500,000 in the next year, you wouldn't say, "I'm going to earn $500,000" and expect to do that overnight, right? You would go to work on earning a certain amount of money every single day until it added up to $500,000 so you could accomplish your goal. Taking small steps consistently will allow you to realize great rewards over time.

8. Review Your Progress at the End of Each Day and Prepare Yourself for What Comes Next.

At the end of each day, invest a few minutes in reviewing what you have done throughout the day and see whether you are closer or further away from your goals. You should be closer, but some days the progress will be minimal. Going back to the idea of preparation, process and production, remember that reviewing your activities will allow you to better prepare for what could happen the next day, so you give yourself the best chance possible to stay on track with your plans. In some cases, this may even allow you to catch up for the time you lost on a previous day. Those days when you can accomplish more are often referred to as being "in the zone" and performing at high levels across the board. Look forward to having more days like that using these steps.

9. Believe in Yourself Even When it Seems Like Nobody Else Does.

When you think nobody believes in you, remember that nobody else knows you as well as you do. That doesn't mean to throw caution to the wind in everything you do, hoping it will work out. What it does mean is that in the words of Les Brown, "You have greatness within you." That greatness requires you to bring it out of yourself instead of relying on others to do so.

10. No Matter How Big or Small Something May Seem, Remember that Everything Counts.

Whenever you are looking at achievements, setbacks, time management, financial planning, learning, teaching, giving, loving, and living, know that everything counts. The fact is that no matter how big or how small something may seem at the time you are doing it, when it comes to meeting your personal or professional goals in all of these areas and more, everything you are doing today will count. It either counts for you or against you. It's up to you to choose which type of activity you'll focus on. You only have one life to live, so make sure that you live it with both the passion and the mindset that everything counts.

Make every internal conversation count by following those 10 steps every single day.

Emulate A Model For Success

Whether we consciously realize it or not, each of us has someone we look up to and admire. There may be many—one or more for each area of interest in our lives. It's human nature to recognize the strengths in others that we seek for ourselves. This shows up in the style of dressing we choose, the cars we drive, where we travel, what we listen to, and the books we read. Billions of dollars are invested in advertising each year to show us what the people we want to be like are thinking and doing.

When choosing someone to emulate, we believe we are capable of achieving what they have become, what they have, or what they do. We use them as a measurement against which to gauge our progress. In emulating a role model, remember that you must do more than change how you appear on the outside. Study what motivates them. Understand the values that they believe in or the internal qualities they have. Why do they do what they do? When you get deeper into this, you will likely find that most have what's called a "chink in their armor." They will have flaws. We all do. Just take what you need from their best and leave the rest. You're not trying to become them. You're attempting to become like them in certain aspects of their lives.

Professional speaker Weldon "Wally" Long is one of the most positive people you will ever meet. When you hear the story of his life, you'll wonder how he ever overcame the bad choices and circumstances he created. To put it simply, he made the conscious choice of changing his internal language—selling himself on becoming a man of integrity who helps others. He listed out the traits he believed were important in becoming that man. He repeated the list to himself constantly and began acting according to that internal language. We highly recommend that you read about how he changed his life in his book, *The Upside of Fear.*

Note that those you choose to emulate are likely changing and evolving as well. They may have their own role models and be working to achieve even greater things in their lives. You may also want to have a role model or models for each area of life in which you choose to grow.

Getting Started

It does take some work to turn this around when your internal language has been committed to a less-than-positive pattern for years. Consider involving a partner or buddy to help you with this at first. When you're exchanging stories about your woes or challenges, ask them to remind you to take the lesson and move on. It can be as simple as having them say, "And how will you handle that differently the next time it happens?" When you become solution-oriented instead of being challenge-confined, your life will change dramatically for the better.

To get a jump on changing your internal dialog, consider writing a series of affirmations you'll say to yourself every day. What do you want to sell yourself on about yourself? Write your affirmations as if you've already accomplished what you speak of, and you'll sell yourself on being and acting as if you have.

Below are a few examples you are welcome to use as a starting point.

> "I take full responsibility for my actions and my life. My well-being is in the best hands it could possibly be in: my own."

"I am a winner. I am a contributor. I am an achiever. I believe in me."

"Today, I'll meet the right people in the right place at the right time for the betterment of all."

"I am a good person. I care about the needs of myself, my loved ones, my neighbors, and my clients."

"I take good care of the vessel called 'my body.' I make wise choices when it comes to fueling my body, exercising, and resting."

"I avoid negative people and gravitate toward those who are positive and successful."

You will want to be more specific than that when developing exact traits or skills that will improve your life, but you get the idea.

What Makes You Happy?

In general, what makes people happy is doing what they enjoy, spending quality time with the people they love, and making a difference in the world. Happiness can be measured in many ways, but focusing solely on financial gain and getting ahead will not produce true happiness. Think about when you were a child and were happy. You didn't have the ability to earn any real money. You didn't own a lot of stuff. Things were pretty simple for the most part, right? And, yet, you probably experienced some of your happiest times during your childhood.

Once we focus on trying to be successful, we can miss real opportunities for happiness that just require us to be ourselves. Albert Einstein once said, "Try not to become a man of success, but rather try to become a man of value." That statement shouts out to all of us that creating value brings great satisfaction and happiness outside of any traditional definition of success.

Albert Schweitzer got this right when he said, "Success is not the key to happiness. Happiness is the key to success. If you love what you are doing, you will be successful."

Defining Success

It's important to note the definition of success isn't the same for everyone. The word is a general descriptive term that could be substituted with "accomplishment," "victory," and any number of other choices. Do any of those words generate a clear picture in your mind? No. That's because there's no context.

- Success for a 10-year old might mean getting a good grade on a vocabulary test.

- Success for a teen might be passing their driver's license exam.

- Success for a college grad might be landing their dream job.

- Success for a sales pro might mean helping a certain number or type of client, earning a particular income, or winning a sales award.

While it's likely that success might be defined similarly for you and others in your group of friends (after all "birds of a feather stick together), the range of definitions can be as broad as the number of people there are on the planet. What's important is to create a very clear picture of what success means to you. Once you develop your definition, you'll find it rather easy to motivate (sell) yourself every day on doing what's necessary to achieve that success. It's important to note that your definition of success may change over the course of time, and that's okay. It probably shouldn't be carved in stone. After all, you'll be growing and changing your whole life.

One of your authors has taught a definition of success for decades that goes like this: Success is the continuous journey toward the achievement of pre-determined, worthwhile goals. With this definition, there's no "arriving." That's because we are continually growing and changing as individuals. Like the different age groups mentioned above, your definition may change and grow as you do. What's important is that you keep re-defining it, so you have a current definition in mind that you're working with.

What if your definition at age 20 (and single) included earning $50,000 per year? Do you think that amount would change by age 30 when you might be married and have a young family to support? Sure, it would. As your life journey changes, so should your goals for success.

The word *pre-determined* in the definition above is very important. Pre-determined means you've given your goals some serious thought. You've created a plan for achieving it and set a course to get there. You have your self-talk written out and are selling yourself several times each day on achievement.

The term *worthwhile* is important, too. This means that you believe in the value and importance of your goals. If you don't set goals that are believable and worthwhile, you won't do the work necessary to achieve them. When you set goals, you *think* you want versus *knowing* you want, but don't really believe you can have, it can cause you nothing but stress and worry, and could lead to disaster.

Who Have You Let "Sell" You?

Most of us have been sold ideals and values by our parents or other relatives. We've been influenced by teachers and friends, bosses, and the media. We are bombarded with messages daily to be, do, or have this, that or the other thing. Vote for Sam! Vote for Sue! Own this brand of perfume and find romantic love. Own this vehicle to create incredible memories for our loved ones. It's happening to us: All. Day. Long.

As an adult, it's important to evaluate what you believe in and why. Who influenced you to believe that the only way to eat a steak is to have it cooked "well-done?" Who taught you that you should keep your old clunker until it flat out dies on you rather than getting a newer vehicle? Who taught you the various stereotypes that you believe? Think about it. What do you believe, and who sold you on that?

Many of our values and opinions were formed when we were relatively young and malleable. Think of your past teachers both in and out of school. Did a teacher or coach tell you that you had a special talent? Has that message led to or influenced your choices as an adult? If those choices have led to positive experiences or satisfying work, be appreciative of what they "sold" you on. If not, let go of their advice and be willing to seek out advice from someone who has done what you want to do.

Once formal education is over, you will likely come across amazing people in every industry. Lessons can be learned from all of them when you pay attention. Some lessons will be what to avoid in your own life. Other lessons may inspire you to do something positive you hadn't ever thought of. Remind yourself that developing yourself is critical versus allowing yourself to wallow in complacency. When we are complacent, we settle into acceptance of being, doing, having less, and those negative voices in our heads will take over by telling us, "It is what it is." Or "Why make the effort for more? This is good enough." We doubt "good enough" is really all you want out of life.

How to Get From Here to There

Begin working on a presentation to sell the most important person in your life—yourself! Create a list of benefits you'd like to enjoy in life. Then, create the plan for their achievement. Sell yourself on the fact that you deserve them—that you can have what you set your mind to and are willing to work for. Continue to grow and develop yourself so, in the end, your life will be an example to others to follow—those who also want to be, do, and have more. Consider the words of Benjamin Franklin in which he shared that, "Without continual growth and progress, such words as improvement, achievement, and success have no meaning."

Have you ever wondered how it is that two people who sit side-by-side at a training event leave with different perspectives on what was delivered? The same applies to those reading the same book or listening to the same podcast. They all received the same message. They all invested the same amount of time. They were all interested in improving their skills. Yet, some take the knowledge, apply it and achieve more for themselves while others do not. What makes the difference is more than their intelligence or even their desire. What makes the difference is what we've been talking about in this chapter: Their belief in themselves. They believe in themselves as champions and do what champions do. They don't set limits on themselves and take in every learning experience with the intention of acting upon it.

When you think of people who are the top in their respective fields, do you see them sitting back and admiring their work for long, or do you see them constantly looking to improve themselves and those around them?

The answer is obvious.

True professionals never stop learning. When you approach every day with the goal of inspiring ("selling") yourself through internal communication, you can achieve your "personal best" level of success. If you are willing to do that, we believe that you will get better and better in the areas you really want to be successful, and that will translate both in your personal and professional life. That's what you really want, isn't it?

Modern-day philosopher Jim Rohn told a story about how he would go to his mentor and complain about how little money he was making. His mentor asked him about it, and Jim said to him, "You see this paycheck? This is all my company pays." Jim's mentor then asked him, "Do other people in your company earn more than you do?" Jim thought about that and answered, "Yes. Some people in my company earn more than I do." His mentor then said, "Then that isn't all your company pays. That's all your company pays *you*." Think about that for a minute. Is that the situation you are in currently?

Remind yourself that you deserve everything you decide that you deserve. Nobody else can ever decide for you and act upon your goals and dreams like you can. Selling yourself on doing something every day that will improve your skills and abilities, so you can have more in your life is always your choice. Instead of waiting or watching, make the choice to act. Remember, your internal communication where you use the language of sales is exactly that, *internal*.

Nobody can hear what you are saying when you are using internal communication but you, so be bold in what you tell yourself you can do and then sell yourself on taking action. Use phrases in your internal communication like, "I am capable of being anything I set my mind to, and nobody can stop me when I believe in myself and my goals. I am a champion in my life, the lives of the people I love, and the lives of people I have never met, as long as I am committed to being the best of which I am capable." Nobody can stop you from being your best in every area of your life but you! That is what gives you the power to decide and act on everything you want to have happen in your life. The only things that can stop you are reasons and excuses, so let's eliminate both of those right now. Focus on creating results so you can achieve what you are determined to achieve.

Your internal communication and your ability to sell yourself to focus on results are going to be paramount to the journey that you embark upon to accomplish whatever you desire in your life.

The thing to remember is that there will be challenges as you start doing things differently than you have in the past. You're exchanging old habits for new ones. Remember, though; success is a journey, not simply a destination.

If you are able to use your internal communication and sell yourself on the journey of being dedicated to being your best, becoming or continuing to improve your ability to be a lifelong student, and never again settling for giving reasons or making excuses, you are already well on your way to accomplishing everything you want to accomplish. Nobody can take away your desire to be better, but desire isn't what will make that journey take you to the places you want to go. The actions you take every single day based on your internal communication will be what take you where you want to go.

10

THE HEART OF COMMUNICATION

"If you talk to a man in a language he understands, that goes to his head. If you talk to him in his own language, that goes to his heart."

—*Nelson Mandela*

What is the true message you are trying to deliver to clients and loved ones alike? For most of us, it's a message that we care, that we want to trust and be trusted, that we want to be helpful, and to enjoy the time we share. That's the language of sales. It's where we mentally remove our own needs from the equation and focus on the needs of others. Doing so helps us to get past the most common challenges faced in communication.

Think about people you know who speak the same language you do. How often have you misinterpreted what they said? How often has the opposite occurred where they misinterpreted what you said? Probably more often than you care to admit. That's because prior to reading this book, you were communicating strictly from your point of view. Hopefully, by now, you have begun to look at things from the other parties' points of view and are starting to have more positive and rewarding conversations.

The biggest challenge of all until now may be that you weren't using the language of sales to close the gap in understanding between you. That will no longer be an issue because now you are able to rely on the knowledge you have gained. You are now capable of making dramatic strides in the areas of understanding how communication barriers can be broken down quickly and easily by using your sales skills to properly greet someone new, build rapport through questions, learn about the other person, and create value for them in the conversations that ensue.

Your messages can be used to either positively or negatively influence the receiving party or parties through your delivery. This is where using selling skills becomes the most valuable to you. Whether you are using this to influence yourself or to influence others, you have to carefully evaluate each situation, so you have the best chance of obtaining the desired outcome. Oliver Wendell Holmes, Sr., stated that you should, "Speak clearly, if you speak at all; carve every word before you let it fall." There are a number of ways to do that, so you are not missing opportunities.

Preparation is the Key to Success in All Selling Situations

As we have explained, it is important to prepare yourself whenever possible for meeting someone, so you have a clear picture of you how you will approach the person, your greeting, your handshake, questions you will ask, information you will share about yourself, how you will carry yourself and your body language, and how you will close the conversation so the person walks away feeling good about him or herself, any decisions they've made, and about you. Whether these are personal or professional meetings, the idea of being prepared should still be at the top of your mind.

When interviewing for a job, consider yourself to be the product you're offering. Plan how you'll present your skills and what those skills can do for the company. Practice your introduction, the first few words you'll say, and how you'll build rapport with the interviewer. Develop some pertinent open questions to get the interviewer to elaborate on information you need in order to determine if this is a good match for you. You'll only want to close them on hiring you if you feel the decision is good for both of you, right?

Use a similar strategy to win over your co-workers. Be truly interested in them and their needs at work. Many a sales pro has increased their success by creating positive relationships with those in customer service or shipping. When your existing clients call in with challenges, you want to know as soon as possible and follow up to ensure their needs were met. If the challenges persist, perhaps it's time for them to consider a newer, larger, better product, and you'll want to be the first one they speak with about it. You wouldn't want to let them be swayed by the competition if you can fulfill their new needs quickly and easily.

And, of course, you will use the selling skills in this book to find, connect with, qualify, and close sales with new clients. If you're an entrepreneur, you may also use these skills to "sell" others on working with you or for you. The same strategies used for moving products can be used to move others to provide their skills for your benefit.

What Selling is Not

The language of sales is not designed to take advantage of others through persuasive communication. It's not a "get-rich-off-others" strategy, though, sadly it has been used by so-called con men and women to dupe people out of their hard-earned money. That's why so many people will be wary of you at first. They'll raise that wall of sales resistance as soon as they know your job title. This is why we are teaching you to be different from the stereotype. In selling, different is good!

Sound selling practices only work well when applied in an ethical manner. As a consumer, making your own purchases, you want to work with people and companies that are truthful, fair, and honest. That's what your potential clients will expect from you and the company you represent.

Speaking of who you represent, take care in choosing your employer. Many a tale of woe has been presented to your authors about the unethical dealings of the companies they work for or even of the managers employed at ethical businesses. If your gut even senses that you could be involved with a less-than-professional business or manager, do your best to do something about it. If you can't persuade them to change their practices, change where you work.

In sales, your reputation may be all that stands between you and a conversation with someone in a legal capacity. You wouldn't want to have it on your resume that you worked at length for a company that ends up making the news in a negative way. In cases where that has happened, employees will often later say they knew something was shady but didn't do anything about it—including saving their own hides. It was easier to stay put than to make the effort to change employment.

Become a Full-Time Student of Selling

The best and brightest in the world of selling study the nuances of selling that are all around them. They see how the people around them interact with each other—noting what works and doesn't work in getting points across or getting agreement. Notice how parents sell their children on behaving in public. Watch how children interact with each other—especially when they first meet. Even better, pay attention to how children lead their parents to decisions. Children are great observers and learn their parents' hot buttons at a very early age. Listen to how servers "sell" the special of the day or enhance their guests' experiences through engagement or encouragement when placing their orders. Pay attention to your co-workers, people on TV, and people in airports. There is communication going on literally all around you. What can you learn from it that you can apply in your own conversations with clients, co-workers, and loved ones?

We can't tell you how much the concepts and techniques presented in this book can enrich your life. Re-read it often with this idea in mind, and you'll find new insights each time you do. Be willing to pay the price ("make the investment"), and you will reach your goals.

Represent Your Best Self

Using the language of sales is ultimately about representing your best self to yourself and to others in every area of your life. Don't you find that when you are feeling your best about yourself that you just perform better? When you are feeling your best about yourself, doesn't that come across to others?

What selling skills will continue to provide for you is continuous improvement. With continuous improvement, you will get better and better results from your communications, which will make you feel better about yourself. That alone will provide a tremendous amount of opportunity in your personal life and in your professional life.

Don't be afraid to set high goals for yourself when it comes to communicating well with others. In the words of Les Brown, "The problem with most people is not that they set their goals too high and miss them. The problem with most people is that they set their goals too low and hit them."

Be honest with yourself. Think through the full spectrum of communication types we have explored, including internal communication and external communication, verbal and nonverbal communication, using appropriate body language, and written communication. Which areas are you strong in, and in which could you use some improvement? Choose just one for now. Then go back and re-read that section of the book several times. For most of us, it takes six times of hearing or reading new information before it begins to stick. When you practice the strategies mentally, and then aloud, you will become more comfortable with them—hopefully, comfortable enough to use them with buyers and start benefiting from them.

We recommend that you never stop wanting to improve in any of these areas because, quite frankly, we all struggle from time to time with communication. This could come from having a bad day and using that as an excuse for poor communication with those we love who don't deserve it. Sometimes we might not believe that we are being valued enough in our professional lives, which can lead to a negative attitude and communication that reflects that with our superiors or co-workers. We can even forget how important we are personally to our own success and be extremely critical about our actions and ourselves when we should be building ourselves up.

The biggest takeaway from all of this is to carefully and thoughtfully produce the best messages possible. When you don't, you are risking outcomes that you might never imagine. You might think things are going along smoothly because there are no apparent challenges during conversations with others, but part of that could be because you are not asking enough questions or communicating frequently enough to know the difference.

This can lead to some of the following examples that could be avoided using the tools you now have at your disposal through effective communication skills.

- Maybe you are not spending time communicating with and learning about what is important to your kids because you live in two different worlds.

- Maybe you are afraid of talking to your boss about a promotion and/or a raise because you don't communicate often enough to even know if your job is secure.

- Maybe you are struggling in your relationship with your significant other or spouse because you aren't connecting in your communication each day, and that is causing you to grow apart.

- Maybe there is a slight language barrier with one or more of your co-workers or neighbors, and you haven't taken the opportunity to make strides in better communicating with them.

- Maybe your clients are considering switching to the competition because you haven't communicated with them recently.

As you think about all the opportunities that exist, remember you can never know too much or be too good at communicating. When you think of the champions in every area of life, what do they have in common? They are constantly seeking ways to improve. You would be well-served to have the same mindset here.

Embrace the communication skills used in sales in every part of your life. Remind yourself every day that people can get information almost anywhere, but what they can't get anywhere else is you. We have been telling you that you are unique and amazing in your own ways, and nobody else out of billions of other people will ever be exactly like you. With that said, don't take for granted what you know now or who you are now as you continue to evolve into being your absolute best self.

In all the examples we have provided of quotations about language, notice that none of them refer to it needing to be a *foreign* language. Language is about communication at both the most basic level and at the highest level. In fact, the writer William Gibson noted that, "Language is to the mind more than light is to the eye."

When you wake up tomorrow, stand in front of the mirror and ask yourself, "How can I maximize using my selling skills, knowing what I now know, so I can bring more value to everyone I meet?" Keep practicing these skills and strategies so you become the absolute best version of yourself. By doing so, we are extremely confident that it will bring you happiness and success in every area of your life.

Let's review what we have covered. To sum it up, *selling is what you say and how you say it.* Even the greatest words and questions are lost if delivered with the wrong tone of voice or with poor body language.

You, as a salesperson, need to know how you sound and look to your clients, even if you have to ask. That's right. If a buyer doesn't buy, ask for their advice on how you can improve. If you are lucky, someone may be honest. Their answer might hurt your feelings but help your income.

As you get better at asking questions, you will begin to exude an unassuming confidence that portrays a modest, but dynamic quality that people want to be around. You are a salesperson, a professional problem-solver, just looking for problems to solve for buyers. Does this sound like the type of person you would like to buy from or know? Most of the great salespeople have an air of quiet confidence about them that inspires others to act.

ABOUT THE AUTHORS

Andy Eilers, MA, CMC

 Andy is a national best-selling author, including award-winning contributions to *In It to Win It* with Tom Hopkins, *The Secret to Winning Big* with Brian Tracy, and *Successonomics* with Steve Forbes. Andy also wrote and recorded an audio program with Tom Hopkins titled, *Ask Yourself This... How Can I Create a Better Life?*

Andy's latest book, *Follow Your Passion and Live Your Life*, has become a huge hit with his followers as a personal and professional development guide for people from every walk of life. Andy was also able to be an executive producer on the Daniel "Rudy" Ruettiger documentary called, "Rudy – The Walk On." This allowed him to work directly with Rudy on and off the campus of Notre Dame to produce and continue to tell Rudy's incredible story throughout the US and abroad.

Andy continues to be a student of people and the sales process by approaching every opportunity to work with others as a learning and growing experience for himself and his team at Andrew J. Eilers Consulting, Inc., and National Sales Solutions.

Tom Hopkins

Tom Hopkins is world-renowned as "the builder of sales champions." His proven-effective sales strategies have helped millions of sales professionals and business owners in industries to serve more clients, make more sales, and earn millions in income.

Tom got his start in real estate sales when he was just 19 years of age. After an initial period of abject failure, he started learning the communication skills that, within seven years, made him the #1 real estate agent in the US.

His client list includes the likes of AFLAC, 24 Hour Fitness, Best Buy, State Farm Insurance, Kavo, Eli Lilly, REMAX, Primerica, and many others for whom he has customized sales training courses. Tom still takes to the public stage for training, offering 2-day Sales Academies annually, as well as touring in Europe and Asia.

He has authored 19 books, including: *How to Master the Art of Selling, Selling for Dummies, When Buyers Say No* and *FILL YOUR FUNNEL - Prospecting with Social Media.*

CPSIA information can be obtained
at www.ICGtesting.com
Printed in the USA
LVHW050141121220
673994LV00003B/3